CIVIL WAR GHOSTS OF ATLANTA

CIVIL WAR GHOSTS OF ATLANTA

JIM MILES

Haunted America

Published by Haunted America
A Division of The History Press
Charleston, SC 29403
www.historypress.net

First published 2013

Manufactured in the United States

ISBN 978.1.62619.190.7

Library of Congress CIP data applied for.

Notice: The information in this book is true and complete to the best of our knowledge. It is offered without guarantee on the part of the author or The History Press. The author and The History Press disclaim all liability in connection with the use of this book.

For the other Miles family: Ray, Wave, Susan, Adam and Bubba.

CONTENTS

Introduction

Federal forces made steady progress in defeating and occupying the western part of the Confederacy. Union victories at Shiloh, Perryville, Vicksburg, Stones River, Lookout Mountain and Missionary Ridge secured Tennessee and Kentucky and possession of the Cumberland, Tennessee and Mississippi Rivers, effectively severing the Trans-Mississippi from the remainder of the Confederacy and taking possession of portions of Arkansas, Louisiana, Mississippi and Alabama.

From Chattanooga, Federal generals U.S. Grant and William T. Sherman considered Atlanta, one of the Confederacy's last remaining major industrial and transportation centers. Conquest of Atlanta would threaten other important portions of the shrinking Confederacy: Columbus, Montgomery, Mobile, Savannah and Charleston, as well as Augusta, Georgia, and a route north through the Carolinas to join U.S. Grant in the struggle against Robert E. Lee and the Army of Northern Virginia.

Grant decided to travel to Virginia and take personal command of the situation there, while loosing Sherman and his Army of the Tennessee on Atlanta and any subsequent targets.

Sherman was opposed by General Joseph E. Johnston and the Confederate Army of Tennessee. The opposing armies fought spirited actions at Dalton, Resaca, Adairsville, New Hope Church, Pickett's Mill and Dallas. Johnston was best on defense, but Sherman had twice his numbers and flanked the Confederates, forcing them to withdraw one hundred miles to the area of Cobb County. There, Johnston found defensible terrain, and bad weather slowed Sherman's forces to a crawl.

In Cobb County the major battles began, not just Kennesaw Mountain but also numerous smaller yet still sharp conflicts at Pine Mountain, Mud Creek, Gilgal Church, Kolb's Farm, Smyrna-Ruff's Mill and Pace's Ferry.

Johnston hoped to hold the line at the Chattahoochee River, but Sherman skillfully crossed at Roswell and slowly began to encircle Atlanta. John B. Hood replaced Johnston, and battles erupted at Peachtree Creek, Atlanta, Ezra Church and Utoy Creek. A deadly, month-long siege of the city was followed by one more savage combat at Jonesboro, and the Confederates were forced to yield Atlanta. A final fight occurred at Lovejoy's Station.

Years before Cobb County and Atlanta became a battleground, railroads brought thousands of wounded and diseased soldiers there from distant battlefields and camps. The men received care at large hospitals, where many died despite the best medical care possible at the time.

These historic events left metropolitan Atlanta haunted. Kennesaw Mountain retains much paranormal phenomena, as does the battlefield at Jonesboro. Buildings used as hospitals, including the Kennesaw House in Marietta and a former inn in Stone Mountain, contain ghosts who have yet to move on to the next realm. Ground consecrated by the blood of soldiers yields spirited manifestations, even in the most modern buildings. It seems that as the metropolis of Atlanta grows, the number of haunted spots increase. This is the story of Atlanta's Civil War ghosts.

PART I
CIVIL WAR SPIRITS OF COBB COUNTY

KENNESAW

The General and the General's Ghost

Following his failures at New Hope Church and Pickett's Mill, Sherman slid back to his railroad supply line at Kennesaw, which was occupied by Federals for six months. Some say the occupiers never really departed.

The prize attraction in Kennesaw is the General, a steam locomotive involved in the Great Locomotive Chase, but it is not the only relic of the Civil War experience in town. According to Barbara Duffey in *Angels and Apparitions: True Ghost Stories from the South*, residents on North Main Street have reported the acoustic passage of Sherman's army. It happens late on hot summer nights, when people sit on their front porches after the traffic diminishes. First, all normal sound ceases—no crickets or mosquitoes are heard—and then, the clatter of horse hooves sound in the distance. Dogs bark as a troop of invisible cavalry approaches, the sound growing ever louder, and then, the tramp of innumerable marching men is heard.

A disembodied voice orders the army to halt and someone announces that General Sherman is approaching. In the sudden silence, a single horseman approaches, stops as if inspecting the area and then continues south toward Atlanta. His phantom army continues the march, the sounds of cavalry, infantry and rumbling artillery passing and dimming in the distance. A creeping coldness and fog always follow Sherman's passage.

Ghosts, including that of actor Fess Parker, are experienced within the Southern Museum of Civil War and Locomotive History in Kennesaw.

Ghosts at the Kennesaw Museum

Kennesaw historian Harper Harris found the old Kennesaw Museum "mighty creepy" at night. "I hear stuff at night all the time," he told Kathleen Walls in *Georgia's Ghostly Getaways*:

> *I usually keep the radio on and try not to stay that late but in the winter it starts getting dark early. Also when the alarm goes off I have to come in here* [the locomotive room] *and sometimes I find stuff lying on the floor with no logical reason. You wonder, "How did that get there." I know I didn't put it there. And then there's the noise. It's not like voices. It's more like thumping and scratching. One night it was real loud back in that room. I thought someone was in here. I've never seen anything but it's scary here sometimes.*

The Great Locomotive Chase was one of the most daring and dramatic events of the Civil War. On April 12, 1862, a group of Union saboteurs stole the locomotive General at Kennesaw (then Big Shanty) and headed north to destroy railroad bridges on the Western & Atlantic Railroad to cut off Chattanooga from Confederate reinforcements and aid in the Federal capture of that vital transportation center.

The General's conductor, William Fuller, chased his engine on foot, by pole car and on several different locomotives, catching up with the Raiders near Ringgold. His dedication prevented the Federals from doing significant damage to the rail line.

Mere yards from the spot where the General was captured, that locomotive rests in this museum, along with an amazing assortment of other Civil War and railroad displays.

Only recently has the museum acquired a named ghost, apparently the spirit of TV and movie personality Fess Parker, who starred in the famous 1956 Disney movie *The Great Locomotive Chase*. He played the Federal leader, James J. Andrews.

"Every house, historical site and museum I know of boasts about their resident ghost," Mike Bearrow, curator of the museum, told Rebecca McCormick of the Monroe Louisiana *News-Star*. "Anytime we misplaced something or couldn't find what we were looking for, we blamed it on the ghost of Fess Parker. The problem was, he was still alive at the time."

Fess Parker died at the age of eighty-five on March 18, 2010, a Thursday.

"When I came in to work Monday morning," Bearrow continued, "I made my usual rounds to inspect all the galleries, because one of my jobs as curator is to make sure all the lights are in working order."

Everything seemed normal, until he approached the Fess Parker display. "It was dark, dark in that corner. I don't mean dim, I mean dark. By the time I got through replacing spot bulbs and florescent tubes, we counted 11 lights that had all gone out at the same time. No flipped breakers. No blown fuses. We all just looked at each other and said it must have taken Parker three days to get from California to Georgia. And now we've got the resident ghost we used to only joke about."

Reporter McCormick saw a coat worn by Parker in the movie and posted the tidbit to her Facebook page via her BlackBerry. Within a minute, a friend in Florida, Joan Ellis, replied that her husband had donated that coat to the museum

"I bought the coat three or four years ago from a Hollywood auction on the Internet," said Jeffery Ellis, a medical doctor and collector of movie memorabilia. "When I called the museum and told them I had the original jacket worn by Parker in the movie, the curator was like, 'Yea, yea, okay, whatever, I'm sure you do, maybe we can take a look at it sometime.'"

Two weeks later Dr. Ellis drove to Kennesaw with the coat.

"Inside the jacket pocket was the original label from Hollywood Costume Co. with this information on it," Ellis said. "'Fess Parker, Walt Disney Productions, Great Locomotive Chase.' The guy's jaw dropped. After additional research by the Smithsonian textile experts, they learned there were actually three jackets used in the movie. This one was the 'pristine jacket,' used for inside shots and promotional material."

A ghost and an eerie coincidence—it doesn't get any better than that.

This facility is now the Southern Museum of Civil War & Locomotive History.

One of Kennesaw's old houses was used as a hospital. Men were treated inside while others waited their turn on a big porch that wrapped around the building. To soothe the suffering soldiers, a woman would play the piano and sing softly. Today that ghostly concert plays on within the house, with no corporeal musician at the instrument.

In October 2001, an Internet posting by Lizardblizard50 described a Civil War soldier that haunted his Kennesaw home. He was twice seen "kneeling by my bed, either praying or begging." The observer was upset because "I don't know what he wants."

The Great Locomotive Chase was an exciting part of Civil War history. The famous engine General shares space with phantoms and poltergeists.

The Kennesaw Visitor

As a child, Barbara Healy lived in Kennesaw, about six miles from Kennesaw Mountain National Battlefield. On a number of occasions, she described for *FATE* magazine, they "often heard a knocking at the door or the ringing of the doorbell," but when they opened the door, "no one was there."

One night during the winter of 1968, following a snowstorm, Healy and her mother were alone in the house when the doorbell rang. They peeked through the curtains on two windows that flanked the entrance and saw that this time there was someone at the door. The two women cautiously left the security chain on and cracked the door to see "a young man, blond and about 20 years old. He was wearing some sort of military uniform and a long gray overcoat" and "looked disheveled and he was barefoot." The man wanted to talk to Jimmy, with whom he had served in the war. Jimmy "had told him to come by if he were ever in town."

Healy's father, James Lloyd Thomas, a World War II veteran, was called Tommy. Healy's mother angrily replied to the boy "that he was too young to have served with my father" and firmly shut the door.

Moments later, Healy and her mother looked out the windows again, but the soldier had disappeared. There was no way he could have walked down their long driveway to the street in the interval, and he had left no footprints in the snow. Healy wondered whether it had been the spirit of "a wandering soldier from the fateful battle of Kennesaw Mountain."

The Kennesaw Mountain Line

Johnston's Confederates established a long, strong line of fortifications between Marietta and Kennesaw, centered on Kennesaw Mountain. Heavy rains prevented Sherman from working his usual flanking routine, so he prepared his largest attack of the Atlanta Campaign, aimed at a Confederate strongpoint on Cheatham Hill. The assault on June 27 failed miserably. Earlier, a Confederate assault at the Kolb Farm had been shattered. These sites are preserved in Kennesaw Mountain National Battlefield Park, one of America's most popular Civil War sites.

It is the curse of Kennesaw Mountain to be located in the sprawl of metropolitan Atlanta. Roads, suburbs and commercial development have surrounded the heart of the battlefield, thankfully largely preserved before Atlanta spread. On weekends and holidays, joggers, people on bicycles and many families out for a picnic and time in the sun inundate park grounds. However, solitary visitors and those who linger as darkness falls often experience supernatural Civil War events.

Kolb Farm: A Spirit Remains

Michael Norman reported an extraordinary Civil War ghost story in his wonderful book *Haunted Heartland.* Because of his service in the U.S. Army, James Tatum and his wife, Katherine, an accountant, had traveled the world. They first retired to Florida but quickly grew weary of the heat. They wisely relocated to more gentle climes, selecting the historic city of Marietta in which to spend their leisure years.

In 1986, the Tatums constructed their home in Kolb Creek Farms, not suspecting that the area had been part of a bloody though largely forgotten Civil War battle. Located near the Kolb farmhouse, a log cabin and landmark of the battlefield, their home, a modern, two-story house, was anything but spooky.

It was a year before paranormal activity was manifested in the structure. At 2:30 a.m. one morning, they awoke to the call of nature. James used the bathroom in the bedroom while Katherine walked a short distance to a facility off the hall. She left the door open and "saw a man walking down the hall in front of the open bathroom door."

Katherine naturally assumed it was James looking for her and called his name. The figure continued on without reply. She followed the man down the hall, repeatedly calling out, "James," but she stopped at the top of the stairs. She believed he had gone downstairs searching for her, but when she returned to bed, she was startled to find him already there. He would have had to pass her to return to the bedroom.

Katherine told James about the encounter and asked if it had been him. No, he replied, and yes, he had heard her calling his name. James grabbed his gun and thoroughly searched the house, finding every door and window secure. They were alone in their home.

Katherine found it "almost impossible" to sleep and ran over the incident in her mind. She realized that the man's passage had been without sound, not what "you would normally hear whenever someone's walking down the hall." A bright security light had illuminated the being, and she determined it was definitely a male figure; she believes he was wearing a coat and hat.

The Kolb Farm at Kennesaw Mountain National Military Park was the scene of an intense battle. Residents have witnessed Confederate soldiers haunting their new homes.

"He was a solid figure," she said. "I couldn't tell what he was wearing because I was on the dark side of him. He was walking like he was going somewhere, not shuffling. And he was swinging his arms as he went by. Like he had someplace to go."

Katherine was frightened by the encounter, unable to reach a rational explanation for it. She concluded that the figure "was not of this world."

The apparition was apparently the ghost of a Civil War soldier, but on which side he fought is unknown. His sudden death left his presence on the land where he met his demise. The Tatums were relieved that he turned out to be a playful ghost.

A month later, James was improving a pull-down ladder to the attic. He put down a drill when called to dinner and then became engrossed in a TV program downstairs. Katherine went upstairs to lie down and rest. Soon, "I heard the drill," she said. "It was real loud, as though someone was playing around with it, turning it on and off. I thought that my husband was trying to scare me with it."

Katherine ignored the commotion for a few minutes but then ran into the hallway to confront James. He was not there, and the drill lay where her husband had placed it hours before, cold to her touch.

Katherine raced downstairs to explain the situation to James. Again, he searched the house but found nothing.

Several weeks later Katherine was watching television upstairs, when she heard "what sounded like static electricity," a popping sound in the air near the center of the room. She turned off the set and walked around the room. Katherine was unable to localize the source but was alarmed when it seemed to advance toward her.

"I backed up clear to the corner and it came right up to my face," she said.

Katherine ducked beneath the phenomenon and ran to find James, who was unable to detect anything amiss. After this incident Katherine was "quite fearful" of the manifestation in the house.

Within a few days, Katherine and James left for a two-month tour of the Pacific Coast and Alaska, and several weeks after returning, they started packing their recreational vehicle for a visit to Florida. As she placed a casserole in the microwave oven, she felt two tugs on her shirt. Turning around she saw there was no one else in the room—James was outside.

There were two other physical sensations connected with the haunting. Katherine always felt a cold spot in the upstairs hallway, where the "soldier" had appeared, and in a guest bedroom, where "I would feel the hair stand up on the back of my neck." She felt uncomfortable there, "like I was infringing upon someone else's room. I don't linger."

James's first supernatural experience in the house occurred early in 1988. He was an early riser, making coffee and reading the paper while his wife slept. If she needed James, she would ring a little angel bell they kept in another guest bedroom.

One morning, James responded to a ring of the bell only to find Katherine asleep, and later, she denied ringing it. Several days later, James was coming upstairs when the bell rang, but it stopped as he reached the last step. He found Katherine asleep and the bell in its proper place. Returning downstairs, the bell rang again. Katherine thought the ghost was teasing him. At breakfast, James told Katherine that he would not respond to the bell unless they had a code. Katherine agreed to ring the bell three times.

Of course, the ghost intercepted the signal. It rang three times, and when James responded, Katherine was asleep, and the bell was still in its separate room. As he left the room, it rang again. James declared that he would never again respond to the bell, so naturally it never rang again.

James kept a wooden bowl on the bedroom dresser where he placed his pocket change each evening. In May 1988, when Katherine was reading in bed late at night, her back to the dresser, she heard a single coin drop into the bowl, and then other coins, one at a time, followed. She turned around, but there was no one there; the coins continued to fall into the bowl. "It was just as clear and as loud as can be," she declared.

Katherine sprinted downstairs to locate James, but all was quiet when they entered the bedroom.

Their haint was a teaser, Katherine decided. "As long as I'm alert and looking for something to happen it doesn't," she said. "It seems to happen only when I forget about it, or I'm engrossed in something else."

Katherine kept a glass of water and a roll of antacids on a tray atop her bedside nightstand. She had just retired one night, James awake downstairs, when she heard the tray being moved and the glass repeatedly lifted and set down. She decided to ignore the phenomenon to see what happened next. Individual antacid tablets began hitting the tray one after another. "It was like listening to a bunch of rats playing around," Katherine thought. When she moved to investigate, the activity immediately ceased.

Later, the Tatums stayed in the house of friends in Florida for a week while the friends stayed in their home in Marietta. Two months later, Katherine was talking to the husband of the couple and asked if anything unusual had occurred in the house. Yes, he replied, early on the morning of the third night, they were awakened by an electric alarm clock they finally found in the master bedroom. If the alarm had been left on, it should have rung the first two nights of their visit.

"Stories of Civil War ghosts abound at the Old Kolb Farm," wrote former ghost hunter Cheri Mohr Drake.

"We've had lots of activity in Marietta, Kennesaw, and Acworth where there were battlefield sites, Native American sacred sites," Drake told one reporter. "Now we have strip malls and subdivisions and people can't figure out why there's a Confederate soldier staring at them every night."

Cheatham Hill in Kennesaw Mountain Battlefield Park

The Fog of Battle

The Georgia Ghost Haunt Hunt Club descended on Kennesaw Mountain on May 2, 1998. They concentrated on photographing the Dead Angle at Cheatham Hill, where the most desperate fighting occurred. It was a

This field, leading to the Angle at Cheatham Hill experienced the greatest slaughter at Kennesaw Mountain. Clouds of gunsmoke have been photographed.

beautiful, clear day, but the photos taken registered a fog of what looked like gun smoke hanging above the battlefield.

The team returned on the 134th anniversary of the battle, June 27, 1998, and photographed the same position. A close-up of the "foggy" area produced what some claim are the smiling faces of a Civil War soldier and a second phantom.

"The battlefield does not keep its memories to itself," wrote Drake. "The shadows of men hiding in trenches and battlefield smoke over a century and a half old were recorded by our 35mm cameras, so that a quantum waver in a fraction of time is ours to see." She claimed that ghost hunters "are really just accidental tourists."

When Drake walked the Kennesaw battlefield one year later, "Every hair on my body stood up," she said. "I went back the next year and got the exact same results." Some of the battlefield is disappearing under residential developments. As a result, Drake stated, "We're getting stories of the new subdivisions being haunted."

They Remain at the Dead Angle

In his fine book *Battlefield Ghosts*, B. Keith Toney described an incident involving a group of seven twenty-something professionals, men and women, on a group outing one fine day in the mid-1990s.

As dusk fell, they gathered their belongings in front of the Dead Angle, the spot below the Confederate earthworks where a field stretches to a distant wood line from which Federals emerged on June 27 to attack the Southern position.

Starting up the trail to the parking lot, they noticed a strange haze that was enveloping the Confederate line. After one woman commented on the sudden appearance of many fireflies, a man said they resembled small spurts of flame. Sensing movement behind them, from the woods, they turned to see a sizeable formation of men, but the figures were indistinct. Within seconds the temperature dropped noticeably. The seven friends continued uneasily on their way. "Guess the ghosts are restless tonight," one man weakly joked. At that moment, they heard moaning from behind them, followed by a thud and cry of pain. The group raced to the parking lot and departed at top speed. None has since ventured back to the Dead Angle.

"I Don't Wanna Die!"

A similar story was told by Gene "Pappy" Harmon, attached to Company D, Twenty-eighth Georgia Volunteer Infantry, a reenactment group (they also portray Federals). They were part of a living-history encampment at Cheatham Hill on June 26–27, 2000, the 136th anniversary of the battle of Kennesaw Mountain. At midnight, Harmon and half a dozen others, including a young boy, decided to walk down the wooded trail bordering the earthworks to the Illinois Monument.

It was a fine evening, despite the typical oppressive heat of summer in Georgia. Frogs and crickets made their noise, and the group was festive as vintage lanterns and candles illuminated the path. At one point, Harmon "faintly smelled something dead…I feel it was disembodied spirits warning us," he wrote. "Later, on the way back, this putrid odor was overwhelming!"

Several in the group "heard voices and saw dark shapes," but others sensed nothing. Harmon walked to the earthworks at the Dead Angle and felt "the hair on my arm rise as I placed it directly above the sacred trench." At the grave of an unknown Union soldier, the party looked "deeply into the woods and strained our ears. Sounds began to be heard all around us, first a voice, then a scraping. Footsteps were heard above us on the path that we had just come down. There was no one else out there but our party."

Spooked, the group returned to the Illinois Monument and decided to retreat to camp. One group took a longer route by road. Harman told writer Jeff Belanger, "About three or four of the guys ran off in the woods and just went crazy, just absolutely out of their minds and I couldn't keep up with them."

Harmon, three adults and the boy retraced their steps on the trail. A man carrying the lantern put out the light "to see better in the dark," which was "a mistake indeed."

At that point, the boy whispered, "We gotta git outta here! I don't wanna die!"

"Ghosts won't hurt you," Harmon said, but the child moaned more urgently, "I don't wanna die! Please."

Harmon instructed the lad to close his eyes, and the group, clinging tightly to each other, hurried down the trail to camp as the boy cried and pleaded. Safe in camp, Harmon asked the child what he had seen.

"I saw a Union soldier in a tattered uniform with his left arm all torn up," the boy revealed. "The soldier walked by, turned his head and looked at me and then walked into the woods." In the trenches, he "saw the heads of four more soldiers watching us."

At a spot on the trail where wounded Federals were burned by fires, the boy said of the spirits, "They're horrible, they're burned up, they're terrible-looking." In *Ghosts of War*, Harmon told Jeff Belanger that the boy "saw actual ghosts of the men after they had burned. I didn't see any of that, but it was at that part of the trail where this historical event happened."

One of the adults noted that "the night sounds were gone, the night now quiet as death, and so it was."

A Novel Encounter

One day in March 2008, Lois Helmers, a resident of Winder, and Jerry Gunn visited Cheatham Hill. The park was nearly deserted and Lois felt a sadness.

Suddenly, "I saw four Union soldiers in the blink of an eye," Helmers told Wayne Ford of the *Athens Banner Herald* for a story that ran on December 24, 2011. "They looked like you and me. They were not ghostly images. They were there and then they were gone."

The Illinois Monument marks the apex of the Kennesaw Mountain fighting and is the battlefield's ghostly focus.

All four men were carrying rifles and seemed to be standing guard. The phantom soldiers disappeared as abruptly as they had arrived.

"I have talked to other Civil War reenactors who have actually seen very similar things," Helmers continued. "We feel there is some kind of energy in that area."

Helmers and Gunn were inspired to write a historical fiction novel, *The Ghosts of Kennesaw Mountain*, released in 2011.

A team from Hauntedgeorgia descended on Cheatham Hill one night, where they first wondered at "the glowing eyes of deer roaming the open fields." Members photographed blue, multicolored and transparent orbs of light around the Illinois Monument, where two members heard "whispering" from a corner. When the whispering EVP was replayed it "was clear enough to be heard by all."

In an Internet posting, Deborah wrote that she and another person visited the park and photographed two orbs that demonstrated faces. "One looks like an older man with a thick mustache! The other looks like a younger man." The photos were taken near the earthwork battery at the Cheatham Hill parking lot.

Visitors have heard phantom orders shouted out to invisible masses of marching troops in the woods, and ghosts have often been heard and felt around the Illinois Monument. A dark, vaporous figure has often been seen there and below on the slope of Cheatham Hill. The spirit cradles a shattered arm while he prowls the area at night and sometimes during the day. When this vapor approaches, dogs growl and whine.

A paranormal researcher was determined to record EVPs at Kennesaw Mountain. One attempt was made on the slope of Cheatham Hill, where the Union attack was halted. A voice gasped, "HELP!" and four seconds later, what sounded to be the same voice said, "WOODS!" although it was less clear. Another EVP revealed a voice gasping, "Who are you?"

Visitors hear distant gunfire and muffled orders; smell gunpowder, blood and sweat; and see spectral soldiers looking out from the woods.

Greg Tolleson, a member of the Ghost Haunt Hunt Team, toured the battlefield with his family and snapped a number of photographs. On one is visible what he described as "a fried head…a head on the ground. And it kind of had a charcoal look to it." During the battle, gunfire ignited the dry underbrush, leading to a truce so the wounded could be rescued, but apparently all were not.

A ghost hunter named Matt has taken his team to the Dead Angle between midnight and dawn and found the area "absolutely infested with spirit activity." He urges others to "check it out and bring some clean underwear."

I've Got a Bad Feeling about This One

Charles G. Harker, born in 1835 in Swedesboro, New Jersey, started clerking for a congressman when orphaned at age twelve. That relationship brought an appointment to West Point, and Harker graduated in 1856. Soon after the war began, he was appointed colonel of a regiment and then earned a brigade. Harker fought gallantly in the fierce battles of Shiloh, Perryville, Chickamauga—where he held Snodgrass Hill while the remainder of the Army of the Cumberland escaped—Missionary Ridge and Resaca. Always near the front, he had four horses killed under him and made brigadier general. Harker predicted victory at Atlanta, though, he confided in a letter, "all of us cannot hope to witness the triumph which must crown the efforts of our magnificent army."

Before leading an attack against Cheatham Hill on June 27, Harker entrusted his papers to a staffer, saying, "I shall not come out of this charge today alive." The attack ebbed only fifteen feet before the Confederate trenches. When his men wavered, Harker rode his white horse to the front, shouting encouragement. The general was shot from his horse and carried by his men to the rear, where he died that afternoon.

Visionaries

NosesCreekPaul revealed to Ghost Hounds that he was eleven years old at the one hundredth anniversary of the fighting at Cheatham Hill in 1964. He lived nearby and walked across the battlefield that day, but that is not his spooky story. Paul's home was located near Noses Creek at the Dallas Highway, where extensive skirmishing occurred the day before Cheatham Hill, on June 26.

Around that date each summer, "you could hear men in the woods chopping trees and sawing logs," he wrote. "My daddy would tell us it was the saw mill working late…and he would always walk to the edge of the woods and look and come back and say (sorta shaky), 'Yep…the saw mill' and send us back to bed."

In 1960, seven-year-old Paul and his brother were sleeping on a screened porch when the phenomenon erupted again. Paul walked into the yard to see the activity while his brother reported him to their parents. Around midnight, "my daddy came out in the yard I said 'Look daddy…men are camping down by the creek.'"

His father looked, said the men were gigging for frogs and urged a return to bed. Paul's mother and brother arrived and asked what was going on. "My daddy replied, 'The camp fires down the creek bridge…' My mom asked 'What camp fires?' He said, 'They're dimming now…let's all go back to bed now."

In the morning, Paul and his dad went to see, but "the men were gone…we didn't talk about it again until 3½ years ago, right before my daddy died…all he said was…'I saw them too.'" Father and son had the "gift," but mother and brother did not. The area today has been densely developed.

Jason Tranetzki wrote that although Cobb County has become suburban, there remain wooded hills that sound and sunlight barely pierce. In these areas, you can still experience the 1864 fighting around Kennesaw Mountain. Gunsmoke "permeates the air," he maintained; the "terrible" sounds of battle can be clearly heard; and an "icy chill" seizes witnesses. Sometimes, a disembodied voice quietly hushes the living, and then leaves rustle before the sounds of combat ring out.

"It Was There, but It Wasn't"

A man known as Brian M. submitted a Kennesaw Mountain story to Cathe's Ghost Encounters. He and his future wife were exploring Confederate earthworks on Little Kennesaw, but after a few minutes, his fiancée felt ill, and a thunderstorm was approaching. The couple had started the half-mile hike back to their car when Brian looked over his shoulder and "saw something move along the ground" in a strange fashion. He said, "It shimmered, distorted the air like pavement might on a hot day, except it was flowing right-to-left, roughly following the contours of the ground." He did not believe it was a heat effect or "even remotely like fog or smoke." Brian pointed out the curiosity to his fiancée, but she could not discern it.

"The best description I can think of for it is that given by C.S. Lewis in his *Space Trilogy of an Eldil*: 'It was there, but it wasn't.'"

The NPS Does Not Recommend

Several years ago Robert M. and his brother regularly hiked the trails at Kennesaw Mountain in the middle of the night. On one expedition at 3:00 a.m., they noticed a man approaching but thought little of it as they often encountered other nocturnal visitors to the battlefield. When the stranger neared, they saw he was "dressed in mid-19th century attire." Close up, they saw "a blank, somewhat distant face." A few seconds after he passed, the brothers turned for a rear view, but the figure had disappeared without a trace.

See NPS Above

Blatantly violating NPS rules, three friends were playing a game of manhunt late one night on the battlefield. Two of the boys were attempting to elude the third, all three racing through the dark woods, when the two young men encountered a fog that they could see through. They ran into and out of the transparent mist, followed by their other friend, and all three fell to the ground for a breather. They occupied a hilltop above the fog, and suddenly, with no breeze to affect it, "the fog forms a Giant perfect circle…no ends or angles" that extended for 150 yards, one of the youngsters wrote UnsolvedMysteries. The trespassers decided to run through the fog again, but at a distance of 10 feet, they all stopped in their tracks when the fog suddenly thickened. They could not

Night visitors to Cheatham Hill have glimpsed visions of horror in these eroded fortifications.

see 3 feet into the mist, and all agreed that they saw "BLACK silhouettes in the fog." They reversed course but found the fog following and closing with them. The trio made a sharp turn and found the phenomenon turning as well. The pursuing fog trailed them until they exited the battlefield.

Here Be Hostile Spirits

Debbie B., her husband, their son and a friend of the boy left their home in the Florida Keys for a camping vacation across the southeast. While walking a trail at Kennesaw Mountain, the son reported hearing voices and gunshots, and then a sudden storm erupted. The boys were frightened, and all four had a sense of being observed. Rain drove the party to the car, and the boys wanted to immediately depart. However, the parents were intrigued and returned to the battlefield, all the while feeling watched and uneasy. Darkness was shrouding the land when a loud noise like a large tree branch striking the ground convinced mom and dad to beat a hasty retreat. Succumbing to a strange feeling, they returned to the car, where Debbie snapped one last picture of the scene. The four drove back to Florida, intent on additional camping. But Debbie fell ill, and they continued home. The last frame of the Kennesaw Mountain visit showed "a dozen or more anomalies."

According to *Skeletons of the Civil War*, Chad grew up in Kennesaw and spent the summer of 1985 on a maintenance crew at the national park. Transplanted to Los Angeles, he decided to take his family east to meet his mother and siblings.

While visiting over Christmas one year, Chad, who is "sensitive to energy," and his girlfriend, similarly gifted, visited the battlefield. "I have seen a ghost down there and have felt the ghosts and bizarre energies at Cheatham Hill," Chad reported. At a certain point on the trail from the Cheatham Hill parking lot to the Illinois Monument, he was always affected "by an energy."

"Rather, I am met with a presence, or a number of them, as I am sent into a quiet but highly physical and psychic experience; my body feels tingling all over as I walk; a warm rush of energy comes into my body from below and fills into my chest, becoming cold; my skin becomes clammy. I feel somewhat insecure, not necessarily threatened, but I feel extremely vulnerable. There have been moments at various visits when I have been nearly compelled to break down in tears." Chad stated that at no "point of my visit to Cheatham Hill do I ever feel normal," he stated.

Artillery killed scores of men at Cheatham Hill on the Kennesaw Mountain battlefield.

On a hunch, Chad picked up a small twig. "I rubbed it between my fingers and palm and the same tingling feeling came back full-force, as if the tree branch, grown out of the battlefield soil, was charged with the energy of the death trauma." He thinks he may be "a channel for that phenomenon." Upon leaving the park, "I am glad," he wrote. The scene today is peaceful, but "the fields and earthworks belie a seething rage there."

Chad's mother also seems to be sensitive. Of the battlefield park she said, "It is as if we are the ghosts walking among their war."

An Internet posting from Nitrofish described a night spent at Kennesaw Mountain when he felt the presence of spirits. He could "hear bomb shells cracking, and dead moaning, and gunshots."

The Ghosts and Spirits of Tennessee website has reports from witnesses who have heard "cannon firing late at night" at Kennesaw Mountain. Furthermore, the "smell of blood and gunpowder are sometimes encountered."

Locals describe seeing soldiers wandering the battlefield after dark and hearing rifle and artillery fire. Most strange are the stories of phantom deer that race toward you before disappearing.

In the late evening darkness of October 8, 2007, a father and son were driving through the Kennesaw Mountain battlefield when both were startled by the sight of a horse and rider that darted into the road directly in front of their car. "I quickly locked down on the brakes as the horse proceeded to come right in front of us," the father told a reporter for WXIA television. Both witnesses were Civil War enthusiasts and immediately recognized the clothing worn by the rider—it was that of a Union cavalry officer of the 1860s. As if this was not startling enough, horse and officer rode straight through a wooden fence as if it had not been there. "My son and I were both in a state of absolute shock," the man continued, "but we managed to maintain and get on the way home very quickly." Although the witnesses requested anonymity, an interviewer believed they were sober, serious people.

The Haunted Battle Line

Amli Apartments in Cobb County sit on part of a long defensive position known as the Brushy Mountain Line, occupied by Confederate troops in mid-1864. When the residential complex was constructed, portions of the earthworks were preserved on the property, with interpretive markers and a trail that winds through the development.

During Robyn Ratliff's one-year residence, she experienced a number of paranormal events on this old Civil War property. She would find her dog intently watching a spot on the wall or observing something invisible with the same expression as when Robyn was talking to him. At times, he would move his head back and forth as he watched. The dog did not act that way before they lived at Amli or after they moved out.

Robyn was working in a back room when she heard the front door open, items placed on counters and someone walking into the kitchen and puttering around. She thought it was a friend and called her name repeatedly. Receiving no reply, Robyn searched the apartment, finding no one. She called the expected friend, who had said she would arrive in a few minutes.

One day, while lying on the couch and watching a movie, Robyn saw an empty drink can on a coffee table "move in a curve shape about a foot long, from one end of the coffee table to the other," she wrote on ghostvillage.com.

On another occasion, Robyn was in the kitchen and a friend was on the porch, the two separated by the living room. Suddenly, "Every piece of AV equipment I own came on for no reason. The big-screen TV, the DVD player, the surround sound, the cable box, everything! I can't even make it do that!" The machines were operated by four different remote devices sitting on a table with no humans nearby.

The only frightening incident occurred after Robyn had taken a shower and was standing in her closet selecting clothes. "I felt this chilling draft move in front of me," she stated. "I got an eerie feeling, and I felt it again coming from the opposite direction behind me. I got freaked out, grabbed clothes and was standing outside my closet. I felt it go across the right side of my body from a completely different direction. I was putting my clothes on as fast as I could when I felt it go by again on my left side—so it had done a complete cross around my body."

Robyn knew it was not her imagination because the ghostly draft moved a heavy baseball jersey draped on a hanger.

Blackjack John

A number of battles were fought for possession of Atlanta, the most violent at Peachtree Creek, Atlanta, Ezra Church and Jonesboro. When they concluded three months later, thousands of soldiers were dead, and Sherman had captured a vital Confederate city. Today, ghosts bear witness to the carnage.

In July 2000, Misha Kantartzis, her husband, two daughters and two sons rented a large, nearly antebellum (1870s) Cobb County house at the corner of Dallas Highway–Georgia 120 and Casteel Road. There is a view of Lost Mountain, the westernmost anchor of the Confederate Kennesaw line, from the kitchen window.

Almost immediately, the family "started noticing strange things," including what Misha described as a "presence." Believing the feeling was due to a new environment, she kept quiet but observed odd phenomena in several areas, particularly stairs leading to the basement and the yard. A door opened as she approached; windows that were locked open slammed shut; dining room lights flickered; things would be heard moving upstairs when she was alone; and she saw "small blurs of movement out of the corners of [her] eyes, flitting around the same areas of the backyard." When she and her husband went to the back porch to smoke, nearly every time, "it just felt like somebody was watching [her]."

She spotted one phantom only two feet from her in the dining room, a man dressed in a blue Civil War uniform "whom I felt was named John, but with the nickname Blackjack." She also felt "that he was lost and confused about why he was here." It was a fully formed figure, "clear as a bell," and that shocked her. The man wore a cowboy-like hat with a small brim, a symbol in the center and gold cords on his uniform. The apparition "wasn't aware of me," she told Jeff Belanger in *Ghosts of War*. "Almost like I was watching a movie or something. He seemed to be real agitated like he was barking out orders," and he vanished within seconds.

Misha had kept a journal since her second night in the house, and much of the account was published on ghostvillage.com. One of the first entries read:

—

> *Aug 27th—moved in Sat—Something weird about the backyard. Trying to ignore it…weird. Out on the back porch, I felt as* [if] *something were watching me, I can't stand to go out there…In dining room saw a man! Tall, thin, slightly built, late thirties to forties, dark hair. Kept yelling, like in a battle. Really strange. He won't shut up! His name is John; he is not a private, but some type of officer. He was definitely in charge. I think he died here. He is wearing blue though, which means he's a union officer.*

Misha had projected a question to the entity, asking his name, and the haunt "was driving me nuts after I got the name…then he wouldn't stop trying to tell me things…Like the nickname…Blackjack, Blackjack, over and over in my head, all day—one day…finally I just said to him…'OK, I got it, but you have to back off." Misha clarified that John "wasn't yelling the name, it was more like he was yelling out commands during a heated battle."

After Misha's second encounter with John, he "started following me all over" the second floor. She has seen John often, particularly in a part of the yard where he "is sometimes a grayish shadow flit[ting] behind the trees…like he is hiding! It always gave me the impression that he was 'sneaking,' and I used to tell him not to do that!"

In the summer of 2002, Misha was mopping the stairs when "a movement" caught her attention through a window placed at ground level at the foot of the stairs. Looking closely, she said, "To my amazement, I saw a hundred legs, all clothed in blue marching past the window" in the direction of Kennesaw Mountain, two miles distant. Each leg was suspended several feet above the ground. The legs might be a residual haunting, a recording that replays under certain circumstances. The stairwell and landing is "where I always" feel something paranormal," Misha said.

Misha stared until the apparition passed and then raced upstairs to confess all her experiences to her husband and a daughter. The girl had sensed John but seen a second male ghost "with red hair and piercing eyes, and she felt [it] was more aggressive and mean tempered." Also, a decaying smell emanated from the daughter's room. Strangely, only Misha and her daughters have experienced these paranormal activities. One daughter saw a Confederate soldier downstairs.

Misha has attempted to reason with the two ghosts, with some success. After tolerating John a bit, she instructed him to stay outside in the yard, where he had first been sensed. John has generally respected Misha's limits, but the other entity has not. She has tried to suppress this entity with crystals, a dish of salt water and burning incense. Occasionally, John "does still walk through my hallways upstairs," usually late at night.

Misha believes John is "basically a nice guy." When she ousted him, "I told him this was new to me, and I didn't know how to help him yet but that I would try my best."

"The other one is very persistent," despite her efforts to dislodge him from the house. She "dreaded talking to the second one. Something inside me told me to not mess with him." She attempted to ignore the redheaded ghost, "but when he gets too close, I must tell him to back off, and he does."

"On a regular basis I have to go through and clear the area with steaming and then with incense, finally opening all windows to remove the stagnant energy," Misha related.

With encouragement from online advisers, Misha went into the yard and "talked" to John. "He is incredibly sad, and I got the feeling he is afraid to go because of his involvement in the war." She was happy before addressing John, but afterward, it required "an hour to overcome his sadness."

Friends with metal detectors searched the property and found artillery artifacts at the "exact spot where I have seen John." On learning this news, Misha walked outside, thanked John and inquired "if he had anything else he wanted to show me."

One thing Misha found strange was that she and a friend had inspected a number of properties before she decided to rent this one. They rejected several houses due to bad vibes, but although they walked all through this house and the grounds, they detected nothing unusual here.

The owner of the property told Misha that a Union hospital stood across the street during the Civil War. Research revealed it to be the Widow Piety M. Green house. It was also discovered that a division of Federal troopers were there for several days in June 1864, and records indicate that Union soldiers camped at this location for three weeks in May and June. Misha and the girls believe the two ghosts "are definitely Union army related." Some have suggested this is the ghost of Major General John "Blackjack" Logan, and

Armies clashed in deadly combat on these fields. When darkness comes, some soldiers continue their ancient battle.

Misha thought her ghost resembled a photograph of that officer; but he was wounded at New Hope Church and had not rejoined the army at Kennesaw Mountain. Logan, later a presidential candidate who commissioned the Atlanta Cyclorama to strengthen his ultimately unsuccessful campaign, died in Ohio in the 1880s. Perhaps John was one of his officers.

"The activity here is really strong on rainy days, and from summer until the fall," Misha said. Perhaps the spirits of two soldiers who died there linger today, wondering why they cannot go home.

Passing the Torch

Donald Carnes is a Cobb County historian who obtained and restored his family homestead, located near Kennesaw Mountain on Burnt Hickory Road. Late one day, as he raked and burned leaves on the property—"not the kind of setting for hallucination," he said—the front door of the old house suddenly opened, and a farmer, bearded, wearing typical 1860s attire, black coat and a hat, exited and paused as he gazed at Carnes. "Then, he turned as if to lock the door of the house and came down the front steps," he told Diane R. Stepp of the *Atlanta Journal Constitution*. "When he reached the second step he disappeared while I watched."

Carnes did not know the man, but he found his image in an old photo album. His name was Pinkney Hairston, and he was a great-grandfather. Hairston did not live there, but the house belonged then to a brother-in-law. The in-law, an angry former Confederate, was enraged postwar when a Federal rode up to the house for directions. The soldier was murdered. "They never proved he killed the soldier because they never found the body," Carnes said. "But we have it on pretty good authority that he did." Hairston, a lawyer, was a frequent visitor to the house, particularly during that period. The brother-in-law eventually died of alcoholism, but it was Hairston's presence that continued to be felt in the home.

"He only appeared once. It was almost symbolic, as if he were turning the house over to me."

Marietta

City Ghosts

Marietta saw a great deal of Civil War activity. The Great Locomotive Chase started there, and it was Confederate headquarters during the extensive fighting at Kennesaw Mountain. After its capture in July, the city became an important Union supply depot and was strongly garrisoned until November, when selected parts were torched as Sherman started for the coast. A number of buildings around Marietta's square functioned as military hospitals for much of the war, and they have provided reports of ghosts.

Kennesaw House

They Checked In, but They Never Checked Out

Along the railroad tracks in Marietta is the famous Kennesaw House, a three-story, thirty-two-room brick structure built by John H. Glover in 1850 as a cotton warehouse and restaurant. In 1853, the structure, originally four stories tall, was purchased by Dix Fletcher and converted into the Fletcher

House, a restaurant and forty-room summer resort hotel, one of the best in Georgia, which was frequented by those who came for the springs located behind present-day Kennestone Hospital. James Andrews and most of his Raiders checked in on April 11, 1862, to plan their sabotage. They rose in the morning to board a train pulled by the General, which they hijacked a few miles north in Kennesaw. The Fletchers were Union sympathizers, which is why some believe Andrews stayed at that hotel.

The Fletcher House was purchased by Mary Starr in 1863 and renamed the Kennesaw House just in time to witness history. The savage battles of 1863 and 1864 brought an army of wounded and ill soldiers to Marietta, where buildings on the square, including the Kennesaw House, were converted into hospitals. Refugees from fighting farther north also found shelter there. In May 1864, the war entered Georgia. By June, the Confederate line was centered on Kennesaw Mountain, and the town shook to the sounds of battle. After the Confederates were forced to abandon Marietta, the Federals soon arrived. Sherman briefly established his headquarters in the building, while chasing Johnston on July 3, and in November as he pursued John B. Hood into Tennessee. In July, the Kennesaw House was used as a hospital and morgue. The structure partially burned at the start of the March to the Sea on November 11–12, 1864, losing the fourth floor and a balcony. The

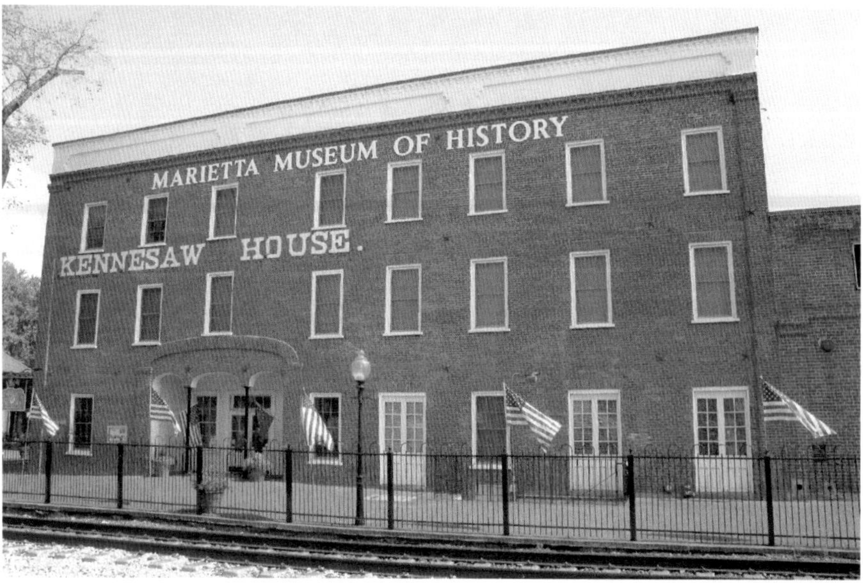

Kennesaw House, a Civil War hospital, has produced a vision of primitive surgery and a ghostly physician.

building was reconstructed as a three-story hotel in 1867 and rechristened the Kennesaw House. Other renovations occurred in 1930 and 1979, and today, the only original parts are the brick exterior, main staircase and walnut banister. The heart-of-pine floors were taken from old boxcars.

The Kennesaw House was once a restaurant, but when it closed, the city of Marietta purchased the building. Since 1995, the Marietta Museum of History has been located on the second floor, exploring the fascinating legacy of Cobb County and the city from prehistoric times to the present. The museum's extensive Civil War collection is housed in the same room occupied by Andrews the night before he stole the General. The space, which contains some of the original furnishings, overlooks the tracks and is the site where the Kennesaw chapter of the UDC was formed on July 29, 1898. There are comprehensive exhibits about the Great Locomotive Chase, the Georgia Military Institute—which stood in Marietta—and the extensive combat that occurred across Cobb County. Featured are one of Sherman's twisted railroad iron "neckties," rifles, pistols, bayonets and accouterments, models of the Georgia Military Institute (GMI) campus and a twelve-pounder Napoleon cannon, locally retrieved artillery projectiles and mannequins dressed as soldiers. There are many other outstanding exhibits and unique artifacts.

THIS DOCTOR STILL MAKES HOUSE CALLS

Some claim the Kennesaw House is haunted by hundreds of different ghosts, and paranormal activity seems to be concentrated in the second-floor museum. The first ghost story might have been reported by a hotel worker who felt a freezing breeze on a hot summer day and suspected the passage of a spirit.

Director Dan Cox and his wife were waiting for the elevator one day in 1994, when an unnatural quiet announced the appearance of a man in outdated clothing. The apparition ignored them before disappearing but left the impression of a person who commanded respect.

"I think I've seen one [ghost] as I've worked here," Cox said in 1994. He believed it was the ghost of Dr. Darrel Wilder, a Union army doctor who treated patients there, including Louise Fletcher, wife of Dix, the Federal sympathizer who owned the establishment during the Civil War. Dr. Wilder was their nephew.

"My wife and I were waiting for the elevator in the lobby of the museum," Cox told Kathleen Walls in *Georgia's Ghostly Getaways*. "I started to chuckle and my wife asked, 'What are you laughing at?' I replied, 'I just saw someone standing beside me.' She asked, 'What did you see?' I said, 'I'll tell you what I think I saw. There was a man standing there. He had on a little flat hat. I call it a riverboat gambler hat. He had a cream colored coat that struck him about [thigh length]. His pants were tucked into his boots.'"

"He looked like a Civil War surgeon to me," Cox told the *Marietta Daily Journal*. Abruptly, the doctor disappeared, "just like a flash of lightning."

"We later found that a Dr. Wilder had come and treated people here. So, anything out of the ordinary around here, we just say Dr. Wilder did it," Cox told Luke Boggs for *Points North* magazine, of the incident.

"I don't believe in ghosts," Cox said. "But strange things do happen here." He also said he believed that when the "Doctor" appeared, it was his mind playing tricks on him.

"When Union troops looted and pillaged Marietta during General William Sherman's occupation," said Connie Cox, Dan's wife and editor of Louise Fletcher's diary, published as *Journal of a Landlady*, "Wilder prevented them from absconding with the Fletcher family's belongings, including a blind horse, flour and pots."

Another employee working alone one day investigated a noise in the hall and encountered a man whose appearance and clothing were identical to that which Cox saw. The being disappeared. At a different time, a second employee also glimpsed the good doctor.

GHOSTS THAT HATE THE STAIRS, AND ONE THAT DOESN'T

The elevator comes and goes without human interaction, usually when Cox is alone in the building working in his office. The elevator stops on each floor and opens its doors to reveal an empty car. It then continues on its paranormal rounds. Cox first witnessed the self-operated elevator during renovations in 1992. He also encountered an invisible entity on the stairwell that stopped every several steps.

Cox's initial eerie encounter occurred one day when he was talking with several men in his office. "We all heard a tapping sound that started on the ground floor and began to ascend the stairs," he told Nancy Roberts, as reported in *Georgia Ghosts*. They thought it sounded like a man tapping his wedding band on the iron railing. Cox opened his door, but the sound stopped. Within a few minutes, the rhythmic tapping resumed, but it ceased when Cox again opened the door. "This happened exactly four times!" he said. Cox descended the stairs to the bottom floor and even stepped outside in an unsuccessful search of someone or something that might have originated the sounds.

Cox has heard an invisible woman calling his name, saying softly, "Dan…Dan…Dan" from a back room while he was alone in the museum, and employees hear unexplainable noises. Among other paranormal activity experienced in the Kennesaw House, Cox added, are doors that "swing open for no reason, and boards creak." One of the moving doors even has "a wedge under it."

"Your imagination runs away with you in an old historic place. It creaks and groans, and it triggers your mind to think of the possibilities. But I've never been frightened. I've never had those cold experiences that I've seen in the movies. And I don't expect to because it doesn't exist to tell you the truth," Cox once told the *Daily Journal.*

"I've heard and seen all types of stuff. When I get here at 6:00 a.m., I hear footsteps. But I don't really believe in that stuff; it's just the imagination," Cox told Carleigh Kate Knight of the *Marietta Daily Journal.*

At night, there are sounds he cannot explain.

Cox once read an old newspaper article that claimed the building was haunted by seven hundred ghosts, but he does not know who made the count or how it was tabulated.

Museum visitors and patrons of the old restaurant have written to Cox, "explaining how they felt presences during their visit," he stated. Cox and Roberts were saying goodbye on the ground floor when the elevator started down from the third floor, opened on the second floor and then continued down, the doors opening in front of them to reveal a lack of occupants. The doors started to close but jerked open as if someone had stopped them with their hands. After a short pause, the doors closed and the elevator headed back up, obeying the commands of its spirit operator and stopping on the second floor. Cox locked up but said there was no telling what floor the elevator would be on in the morning.

"My computer screen faces the door to the museum," Cox told William Bender in *Haunted Atlanta and Beyond*, "and one evening a shadow went across my computer screen. Of course, the outside room was dark and when I looked around no one was there."

SMILE, YOU'RE ON HAUNTED CAMERA!

Cox captured two ghostly white images when he had a color security camera in the museum. The glowing, people-shaped white figures resemble a man in a long waistcoat and a woman with a ponytail in a long dress. "I saw this figure on the TV monitor in the back office," he told Kathleen Walls. "I thought someone was in the museum, so I walked up front and no one was there. I went back and took a picture of the TV monitor." Cox believes the images were caused by the afternoon light shining through windows. Unaccountably, no images have been recorded on a new black and white system.

Walls asked Cox for a good site to photograph paranormal activity. He pointed out a female mannequin clad in an old wedding dress. One picture showed nothing unusual, but a second captured a halo around the figure's head. The intriguing photo is on the cover of her book, *Georgia's Ghostly Getaways*.

Ghosts Cutting Up

The strangest Kennesaw House experience occurred to author Barbara Duffey when she arrived to interview Cox. As related in *Angels and Apparitions*, stepping off the elevator, she "was overcome by a faint vision." At the rear of the large room she glimpsed "a primitive operation." Several attendants helped the ghost doctor frantically in the procedure, which she could not discern because "the scene disappeared too fast." A short, grim girl held a candle to illuminate the surgery. As the ghostly operation faded, Duffey felt "anguish, futility, and intense fear."

Cox's experiences are not restricted to his museum. He was driving near the Kolb Farm at Kennesaw Mountain, on Old Dixie Highway through the battlefield, one night when he turned from a side road and saw a Union soldier standing in a field near a railroad bridge, clutching his musket and observing Kennesaw Mountain.

"I could see that guy," Cox told William Bender for *Haunted Atlanta and Beyond*, "with that musket on his shoulder, standing right next to a tree just as plain as day."

Another Phantom Surgeon

In a *Creative Loafing* article, "The Tales Behind Some of the City's Most Ghostly Places," published on October 27, 2011, Curt Holman quoted Dan Cox as saying, "Until I get slimed, I'm going to be a nonbeliever."

One story from the museum that Holman enjoyed involved a young man in the 1880s who arrived in Marietta to find a bride. The hotel had just been rebuilt, and the man had been given a room on the third floor. He took the elevator up, but when the door opened, he saw, not the modern floor, but a dark room lit by a dim lantern hanging from the ceiling. The suitor saw a doctor looking down at the figure of an unconscious Confederate soldier. The blood-soaked surgeon was amputating a leg, rhythmically sawing at the flesh until the doctor stopped and looked at the man standing in the elevator. The horrified guest quickly returned to the ground floor and fled to take a room in a less haunted establishment. Hotel staff took the lift to the third floor and found everything normal.

Henry Higgins, a Cobb County police lieutenant who had volunteered at the museum, told the *North Georgia Journal*, "I've seen the ghost three times." He attributed the phenomenon to various things—passing trains or car headlights below. "Just about the time you see him, he's gone," the law enforcement officer said.

Annals of the FPR

About half a dozen different groups have investigated the ghosts of the Kennesaw House. In 2001, the Foundation for Paranormal Research (FPR) made arrangements to explore the building one night at 9:00 p.m. Members Chris and Barak Cowling arrived at 8:53, and Chris wrote in her website report that she "immediately got my old familiar 'heavy' feeling in my sternum."

Several hours later, Barak checked the time to find his watch had ceased operating at the exact moment they had entered the building. Mechanisms often stop working in the presence of paranormal activity, particularly battery-powered machines that seem to have their energy drained. Chris noted that it "was only one of several equipment abnormalities that evening." Donna, a colleague, discovered that when she attempted to load thermal film, her camera "would not advance the film in the right direction." However, a roll of ordinary film, less useful for registering ghostly activity, was readily accepted. Barak was taking photos with another camera when it automatically began to rewind on frame thirteen. Dan Cox showed the group his collection of photos that seem to depict misty human figures.

Electromagnetic field (EMF) detectors registered unusually high readings in the main room of the museum, but the most activity indicated was near the elevator, where Cox had noted ghostly manifestations on several occasions. After a motion detector was focused on that spot, it went off in the early morning hours when no one was present in the area.

Chris was drawn to another site of repeated paranormal activity on the stairs, where two mannequins dressed in period clothing play out a scene from *Gone with the Wind*. She had felt "most uncomfortable" there and at the back of the main display room on a previous visit. Again, "those feelings persisted in the exact same areas," she said.

Chris was talking to another FPR member, Olivia Newton, near the top of the stairs when, "I thought I saw a shadow out of the corner of my eye." She took several photos of the area that developed into "some of our more spectacular shots…of mists and vortices."

At the back of the main room, team members were sitting in chairs when "Barak felt a slight brush on his hair," according to the group's report. At that moment, Donna took a picture that revealed a fog near his head. Photos also revealed a wisp and vortex around the front desk, where Chris paused to take notes.

Chris noted that each photographer captured different types of anomalies on their films—orbs, shields, mists and vortices.

The now-deceased Georgia Haunt Hunt Club (GHHC) visited the Kennesaw House on September 19, 1998. Several orbs appeared on photographs of the haunted stairs and near a mannequin dressed in a hoop skirt, in addition to a "shield-shaped anomaly" above a photograph of U.S. senator and Confederate general Robert Toombs. They also recorded "much unexplained EMT meter readings."

On October 17, 2003, six members of FPR, including Olivia Newton and Rick Heflin of the GHHC, returned to the Kennesaw House. Doug Williams set up his camera in the top-story hallway, a frequent site of ghostly activity, and captured orbs that traveled vertically, horizontally and diagonally across the camera screen but were invisible to human eyes. "The movement in different directions will eliminate the possibility of it being dust moved by an air conditioner blowing," he explained to Laura Ingram of the *Marietta Daily Journal*. "We try to rule out anything that would cause it." He theorized that they could be the spirits of soldiers or others who died in the hotel.

Joni Goodin, who first encountered the paranormal at the Kennesaw House, led Ghosts of Marietta, a walking ghost tour of historic and haunted downtown Marietta. She said the Fletcher family had three daughters, and some believe that one of the girls remains today. "I'm not sure why," she told Knight of the *Daily Journal*. "But they did live through the Civil War, a terrible time of tension and death. The Fletchers were Unionists, and it was really a period when families were being ripped apart and women were being left alone."

Many articles have been written about the Kennesaw House, a number of investigations have been posted online and it has been featured in a number of television channels, including the History Channel, CNN and PBS.

Haunt Misbehaving

At 780 South Cobb Drive in Marietta, now located off Pearl Street, west of Dobbins Air Force Base, was one of Georgia's finest restaurants: the 1848 House. In 1848, John H. Glover, Marietta's first mayor, constructed the huge Greek Revival structure as the center of his three-thousand-acre Bushy Park Plantation. On July 4, 1864, skirmishing occurred on the plantation's grounds. The action was known as the battle of Bushy Park and was part of a greater battle at Ruff's Mill. The owner wrote that many soldiers "were killed or wounded near the house." A bullet hole remains in the side of the structure. After the Confederates retreated, the Federals used a second-floor room for operations, and the rest of the house served as a hospital, particularly following the battle of Allatoona in October. The owner allowed Federal officers to stay in the residence, which of course guaranteed that it was protected against harm, although hoof marks remain on the floors. The house has had over twenty owners since the war.

Lillian and George

Many employees of the 1848 House, which retained thirteen acres of land, believed two ghosts haunted the house. Lillian ruled the first floor, George the second. "They don't seem to like each other," the restaurant's homepage revealed, though other observers disagreed. But it also noted that at least they "don't seem to be evil, just mischievous."

The second-story male ghost was thought to be a Union soldier who died in the house or on the grounds. The primary room, once used for grisly operations, was painted blood red and named the Scarlet Room. George's repertoire there included making a heavy chandelier swing in wide arcs, playing red "laser pointer–like" lights on the walls and floors, running clocks backward (consult the Surrency haunting in *Weird Georgia*) and rocking chairs on the front porch. The sound system, which normally played soothing music for the diners, would suddenly start blaring rock-and-roll. The red-dot "laser" was not blocked by tables or other obstacles, apparently shining right through physical objects. The chairs rocked in rhythm during the middle of the day and immediately stopped when someone arrived to investigate. Some believed George and Lillian liked to rock together.

The ghosts had a habit of knocking loudly on the doors of closets. When workers attempted to open the closet, the door would refuse to cooperate. Access was granted only when the banging ceased, and often the phenomenon

This former restaurant in Marietta, utilized as a Civil War hospital, was haunted by a soldier on one floor and a woman on another.

was transferred to another closet, where that door could not be opened until the sound ceased there.

"There was a bright, sunlit day," said Dot Dunaway, "there was no wind going, and all of a sudden my daughter started pointing out front and saying, 'Mommie, Mommie, Mommie' and everyone turned around and on the front porch there were three rockers on that side of the house, and two of them were rocking very purposefully."

She and her daughter "went over to the window and the rocking chairs were as if someone were rocking them very forcefully and very rhythmically, and she said, 'They'll stop in a minute,' and they did." No living person was on the porch.

Patrons and employees alike experienced ghostly phenomena, but few saw an entity. In the autumn of 1996, a guest "saw a woman in a long, old-fashioned white dress with a handkerchief tucked in her sleeve," owner and past Marietta mayor Bill Dunaway told Nancy Roberts. Over a period of fifteen minutes, one patron twice saw a woman looking out a window in the room. Employees outside the house observed the image of a woman in a long dress in the Scarlet Room. Presumably that was Lillian in not quite the flesh. "Several people have seen a woman, wearing a white dress, looking out of the attic window over the drive," Bill told Corinna Underwood in *Haunted History: Atlanta and North Georgia*.

Dunaway told a *Marietta Daily* reporter that he was not certain what caused the phenomenon but added, "I'm not going to stay here late at night by myself and find out." However, he believed "if we have something here, they're not nasty. They might try to scare you, but they're not nasty." He believes events "have happened in the house that I can't explain," but he is not afraid. "They can bother you, but they're not destructive."

One night at 12:30 a.m., general manager Don Couvillion was supervising cleanup when a worker called his and another employee's attention to an electric clock. The clock read 11:00 p.m., and the second hand was racing around counterclockwise. Couvillion also would not admit that a ghost was responsible, but the "clock made me wonder, and I still can't explain it—it was too strange." Afterward the chronometer kept perfect time.

Another employee, Alice Upright, was relaxing with a cup of coffee when she saw a chandelier move. "It was swinging, not just swaying," she said. "I was shocked." The incident resolved her skepticism: "I had to believe after that." Half the staff believed the building was haunted, while others did not.

"One time, I was walking into an upstairs room, and the chandelier was swinging on an arc," Bill Dunaway stated. "That room was the operating room, and lots of occurrences happen there."

Dunaway and his wife had just prepared floral arrangements for a cocktail party to be held that night. She was chatting with two friends when they abruptly fell silent and their eyes widened. Looking behind her, Mrs. Dunaway saw what had dumbfounded them. One flower arrangement was being lifted from the vase by unseen hands and then carefully laid on the table.

Several years ago, the lights took to blinking on and off for no cause until Barbara Tillery commanded, "George, don't do that anymore." George politely complied.

One night, a guest from California told Dunaway that two of his great uncles had fought in the Battle of Bushy Park. The men agreed to speak again the following day, when the visitor asked, "Is the house haunted?" While in the Red Room, he had felt a presence, which remained until he left the room. Dunaway explained that the room had been an operating theater, and the man said that in a diary one of his great uncles had written that he had a leg amputated following the battle. Both agreed the surgery probably occurred in the Scarlett Room.

The Georgia Haunt Hunt Team's October 11, 1998 investigation revealed that the Scarlett Room was probably the most actively haunted room of the house. A GHHT member watched an orb blinking on and off in a corner of the room, and a photograph captured a small blue orb there. Other balls of light were photographed above a dining room chair, hovering beside a chandelier, near owner Dunaway, and in the attic. A face seems to peek out from behind an exterior column, and an orb was caught near the famous rocking chairs. A shot inside the detached kitchen showed two shield anomalies.

The 1848 House has ceased operating as a restaurant and is now a private residence. It gained national publicity after features on both the History Channel and Discovery Channel.

Cemetery Antics

Within Marietta's city cemetery is a large Confederate section, containing soldiers killed in the Atlanta Campaign or who died in local hospitals. Residents tell of seeing uniformed soldiers roaming the grounds at night and hearing gunshots, drumming and marching.

One of Georgia's largest Confederate cemeteries is found in Marietta, where the figures of soldiers have been glimpsed after dark.

During a 1998 GHHC expedition to the Marietta Confederate Cemetery, EMF-meter readings caused members to take photographs that produced a number of anomalies, including mists, balls of light that changed form and a column of white light that extended from a tree to the ground.

Alan J. Levine wrote that after sundown in Marietta, "the old Confederate tombstones bear witness to the cry of a soldier boy who suffered a morphine-less demise defending his home and family on the fields below Kennesaw Mountain."

Conferring Ghosts in the Family Room

Sandra from Marietta and her husband moved to Georgia several years ago, purchasing a four-year-old house that she thought was too "young" to be haunted. One morning, she was alone in the house, working in the kitchen, when she heard men's voices in an adjacent room. Believing a TV had been left on, she entered the family room, and to her "amazement a small group of men dressed in Civil War uniforms was just standing around in a circle, talking in hushed tones." After realizing that she was experiencing the supernatural, "I froze in terror," she stated. One soldier looked not at her, but through her. Horrified, she fled the house.

Since that time, she has again heard the men's quiet voices when she was alone, and "even saw two men quickly appear and disappear in my kitchen and foyer." Sandra learned that her house is located near Cheatham Hill and believes Confederates had a camp nearby and followed a trail to the battlefield. Her home was constructed along the path. They "probably died in battle and do not know it and still carry on forever their daily soldier's duties," she thinks. Understanding their situation now, she finds their condition sad and has empathy for them. "It's no longer scary when I hear the voices," she concluded.

As to why ghosts are invading modern homes, Cheri Drake had a thought: "Georgia has kept relatively few of its Civil War battlegrounds untouched, hence the misplaced spirits who inhabit homes in such unlikely areas as Marietta and Kennesaw."

Houses, apartment complexes and condominiums are constructed over many unpreserved battlefields, hospital sites and graves that most people have long forgotten.

"We get a lot of calls from people who live in these upscale neighborhoods in and around Atlanta," Cheri Drake said, "and they can't understand why their house, built only three years ago, is haunted by a ghost. We tell them it's because their home was probably built on the site of a battleground."

Smyrna and Ruff's Mill

Let's Do the Time Warp Again

In July 1864, as Johnston withdrew from his Kennesaw Mountain line, Sherman hoped to catch and destroy part of the Southern army before it crossed the Chattahoochee River, but Johnston put up two stiff rearguard actions at Smyrna and Ruff's Mill.

In 1972, a resident of Winnipeg, Canada, took a job in metro Atlanta for six months. He lived at a new condo in Marietta, where he saw Ruff's Mill reenacted solely for his benefit.

One night, the man left his condo about 1:00 a.m. for a walk and some fresh air. He was strolling through an open field behind the building when he heard the sounds of battle: artillery pounding, rifle fire crackling and human shouts of excitement and pain. "I froze, just couldn't move," he said.

After several minutes, the scene of battle was revealed. "I saw the images," he stated. "Screaming, cannons, men in gray uniforms not too far away in the distance." Curiously, "all I could see were the guys in gray, not who they were fighting against," and he "even smelled a putrid odor." The man remembered being "alone, but not really afraid." Following ten minutes of the audio, visual and nasal exhibition, "everything disappeared as quick as it appeared; the air was fresh and clean again."

The night was clear and quiet, and the other condo residents fast asleep. "I thought I was going insane," he said. The man did confide in a minister who lived in the building. The clergyman took him to a historical marker a short distance away that described a Civil War battle. "He told me that the condo was built over a Civil War site. I was shocked!" The Canadian knew nothing of the American War Between the States.

"That night in Georgia changed me a whole lot," he continued. "The images and sounds are imbedded in my memory till the day I die."

"What did I witness?" the young man wondered. "Did I see some kind of hologram of the past?" Could be, judging from Cheri Mohr Drake's theory of psychic recordings

Lassie Came Home

The man had another paranormal experience in Georgia, indicating he may be somewhat psychic. An older woman occupied a big house beside the condo. He considered her "eccentric" as she "never trusted anyone and rarely came out." One day he saw her out and asked about the beautiful black dog he had seen in her yard. "I have no dog!" she snapped, but when he described the animal, the woman exclaimed, "Oh my God, that was my dog that died fifteen years ago!"

The Waterheads

A covered bridge stood at Ruff's Mill on Nickajack Creek before the Civil War, but it was destroyed during the fighting. The present covered bridge, dating to 1872, has been reinforced with steel beams and concrete piers. Being a one-lane bridge on a metropolitan road makes it a constant hazard for drivers.

This locale is haunted by "the waterheads," which exist in or near the creek. Residents believe the ghosts are small children, according to Curt Holman in *Creative Loafing* magazine. One historical incident involved the three-year-old son of John Reed. In 1874, according to a contemporary account in the *Marietta Daily Journal*, the child wandered into Ruff's Mill and made it to the top level, where his clothing was caught in the milling mechanism. The paper related that the miller "ascended to the upper floor and to his horror found the child stripped of its clothing, bleeding, gashed and lifeless wedged in among the machinery." Other "waterheads" may include children who drowned in the creek.

The 1.7-mile Heritage Park Trail leads hikers along the creek and mill ruins.

Mr. and Mrs. J. Harold Ivester purchased the Martin L. Huff House in 1976 and restored it. The building had been used as a hospital during the Battle of Ruff's Mill on July 4, 1864. "Oh, the ghost stories we heard while living there," Mrs. Ivester recalled, although apparently nothing unusual was experienced by the couple.

Sope Creek: Dowsing the Ghost

Steve Hudson is a legend in Georgia hiking circles. There are few places he hasn't hiked, and he shares the experiences in numerous books and magazine articles.

In the September–October 1995 issue of *Georgia Journal* magazine, he described a hike along the banks of Sope Creek, which features the ruins of the Marietta Paper Mill, thought to have produced paper for Confederate currency. This is also close to where Sherman first crossed the Chattahoochee, forcing the Confederates to retreat closer to Atlanta. Union cavalry destroyed the mill. Hudson encountered another hiker, whose name, Tom, was prominently displayed on his hat, and he was equipped as a veteran of the trail. The strange aspect to Tom was the wire he carried—it was shaped like an *L*, and he was twisting it in his hand.

Tom asked Steve if he had seen anything of interest. Steve replied that he had seen a hawk and asked Tom whether he had seen anything. The unexpected reply was, "I saw the ghost!" Steve did not know what to make of that. "The ghost. Over there," and Tom gestured. "By the ruins. Old Confederate guy. Seen him a couple of times before. I just kinda dowse him up now and then, like some folks dowse up water. Guess he likes it out here. Worked in the old mill, I reckon."

Steve Hudson had never before encountered a ghost dowser and probably never did again.

The ruins are near the Sope Creek Bridge on Paper Mill Road, in the Chattahoochee River National Recreation Area.

PART II
Civil War Ghosts of Metropolitan Atlanta

Roswell

Johnston expected Sherman to cross the Chattahoochee River downstream, but the Union general skillfully shifted his forces upstream, building bridges at Roswell and breaching the barrier. He destroyed the mills there and cruelly shipped the workers north. Many never returned. Just before the Federals continued their final advance against Atlanta, a lightning storm of biblical proportions struck, killing men and discharging loaded muskets.

According to Dianna Avena in *Roswell: History, Haunts, and Legends*, in the early 1990s, an antebellum apartment block called the Old Bricks was renovated for the Founders Club and could be rented for events. The décor was Civil War themed, with the structure and property protected by a sophisticated security system that featured motion detectors. Dueling prints—one of a Confederate soldier, the other a Union warrior—were placed on opposing mantels. On the morning following their installation, the picture of the Federal was found on the floor a distance from its mantel, face up, the frame undamaged but the glass shattered, seemingly stomped by a boot heel. The security system had not detected anything amiss.

This obvious Confederate presence was dubbed by members and employees as Fred, which manifested itself as a prankster. Several years after the print vandalism, a club member was regaling a group with stories as they all sipped drinks. Abruptly, an invisible force lifted the orator slightly off his feet, rotated him halfway around and gently set him down, to the consternation of all.

Workers found the kitchen area a refuge from Fred's jokes, but the second floor, on the opposite side of the complex, was his domain. One night, a supervisor and two workers had prepared that area for a luncheon—seven tables, with six chairs at each, had been arranged, with silverware, plates, glasses and napkins. After the three returned to the kitchen, the supervisor ran upstairs and found the chairs at one table pushed back, a napkin draped over the back of each seat and the silver crossed on each plate. This became such a frequent phenomenon that the room was checked immediately before an event.

In 2005, the club closed, and the Old Bricks received an extensive renovation—the building was gutted and expanded with new construction to form condominiums. Avena found the site even more active during this period, but with a new presence—a young female child. That fall, Avena took a group on her Roswell ghost tour to the Old Bricks and addressed them with her back to the structure. "I began to feel an intense cold on my back," she wrote, when a man shouted that an upstairs window was opening. They all watched the window continue to rise and noted that

These apartments, since converted, were built for millworkers in Roswell. A ghostly child has been seen in windows, and a restaurant was plagued by poltergeists.

the building had no flooring. As Avena backed away, she heard "loud, clunky footsteps approaching me from behind." Whirling around, she saw no one.

On a November tour, a college student was shooting video for a class "when he suddenly yelped and jumped backward." Thorugh the viewfinder of his camera he had seen a young girl staring at them from a downstairs window. The child was invisible to the naked eye, but when the tape was replayed, everyone saw the girl, who popped up into the window, stared at the party and then disappeared.

On other occasions at the Old Bricks, Avena was pushed off a step and felt her left thigh grabbed from the rear. Guests felt invisible entities grasping for their hands, and one felt a presence playing with her hair.

At Old Bricks in January, Avena was with a group of fifty middle schoolers from Florida when every kid gasped and pointed in unison—they had all seen an eight-year-old girl walk into an empty door frame, turn to stare at them and continue on her way. Suddenly, the group screamed, turned and ran toward a busy intersection. Avena and the chaperones safely intercepted the young people, who gasped out their story—the girl had repeatedly passed the door, but on her fifth appearance, she "bolted out toward us."

The Voila Hair Salon, on Sloan Street in Roswell, was a duplex constructed for millworkers around 1840. According to Avena, two women may have suffered tragic deaths there because of the Civil War. One woman was murdered by Federal soldiers, and the second, learning that Sherman was removing every woman and child from the town, slit her throat in front of a hearth. A number of people have seen a lady standing beside the fireplace, and another woman, clad in a ball gown, makes appearances, particularly on the stairs. The house has cold spots, and no one is comfortable upstairs at any time. One employee could not plug in a hair dryer without it blowing up.

One morning, with the salon closed for an employee class, all workers heard a loud impact upstairs. Investigators found that a trash can lid had come off and leaped several feet to land on the floor. When the Georgia Ghost Society investigated, a sensitive detected a woman upstairs pacing back and forth. Two investigators with a magnetic field detector were startled when their meter went off the scale five times, separated by up to forty-five seconds, which corresponded with the pacing of the ghostly woman.

Avena described another house, since converted into law offices, that is modern but occupies the site of a millworker's house. One day, a woman, thinking she was alone, spotted someone sitting in a posh chair. Sticking her head in to say, "Hello," the woman saw the chair pivot and "a man in a Confederate soldier's uniform" occupying it. The man made eye contact before disappearing. The law firm experienced considerable trouble with the computer in that office. Three times the occupant of the office denied the existence of ghosts only to find his hard drive wiped clean the following morning. Three different computer companies failed to find any problem.

The lawyers had folded their tent and relocated when Avena took a tour past the building. One woman asked, "Are there Civil War reenactments taking place around here?" which is the kind of question that delights a ghost tour operator. Several sisters "had just seen a man in a Confederate soldier's uniform pacing back and forth inside that office," Avena wrote. A week later, a group with her saw a man "with shiny buttons up on his shoulder"—surely another soldier sighting.

Michael and Katherine, Together Forever

The Roswell Mill Commissary, located on Roswell Square in front of the mills, is a brick structure that was built in 1854. Here millworkers purchased their necessities; at least until Confederate forces transformed it into a hospital, later taken over by the Federals. It became a general store, then a funeral home and, later, the Public House Restaurant. It became a J. Christopher's restaurant, and is again the Public House where many members of the staff have reported paranormal activity. They credit the hauntings to two ghosts—Michael, a seventeen-year-old Union soldier who died in the hospital, and Katherine, believed to be a young Southern woman, possibly a Confederate nurse, clerk for the commissary or millworker, who fell in love with the Federal and also managed to meet her fate there. Michael may have been killed on the square outside, perhaps hanged—either because he was found being amorous with Katherine or in reprisal for Union crime—despite Katherine's pleas that he be spared. She soon died, we presume from a broken heart, although some versions have her witnessing the execution from the upstairs window of the restaurant and committing suicide by hanging from one of the second-floor rafters in that room. One variation has Michael killed during the terrible lightning storm and washed away in the nearby Chattahoochee River and Katherine vanishing several days later.

The Public House restaurant might be the most haunted building in Atlanta.

The spirits are apparently inseparable. When the restaurant is opened, staff members have found a corner table with crystal, silverware and napkins moved. At a piano bar upstairs, from which loud crackling noises have emanated, two chairs that are always left facing into the room will be found in the morning at a window overlooking the square. Some believe the cursed lovers dance there (and they have been glimpsed in that activity), and others believe they enjoy just sitting in the upstairs room watching activity in the square. Some citizens have reported a figure walking around the darkened second story carrying a candelabrum.

Several staff members have sensed Katherine at the top of a flight of stairs, and one man saw a female apparition there for several seconds before she suddenly vanished. Wangler also wrote of witnesses who have seen a young woman clad in a blue antique skirt.

One day around noon, the owner was near the windows when the shades abruptly shot up in sequence, from one end of the room to the other, as if a ghostly presence wanted a sunny exposure.

In *Ghost Stories of the Civil War*, Dan Asfar and Edrick Thay quote Mary-Alison Wilshire, who worked several summers at the Public House while attending college. In the restaurant, "you kind of felt like you were never by yourself," she said. Before opening one evening Mary-Alison checked the women's restroom, but when she returned five minutes later, all the lights were out. She turned them on and searched the area, finding no one. As she prepared to leave, a toilet flushed. "I think the ghost was playing tricks on me," she said. On another night she lit all the candles on the tables, left for a short time and returned to find them all extinguished.

Another women's toilet story was told by Dianna Avena in *Roswell: History, Haunts and Legends*. A number of women report that while they attend to business in a stall, the hooked-latch lock will lift in front of their eyes and the door thrown open to reveal no person outside. Also, while washing their hands, they see in the mirror a middle-aged woman with short, blond, curly hair. Of course, when they turn around the woman has vanished.

On yet another night, hostess Mary-Alison distributed pagers to patrons waiting for tables. Suddenly, every pager spontaneously lit up and started vibrating. Annoyed, she unplugged the mechanism that activated the pagers, but it made no difference.

Of Katherine and Michael, Mary-Alison said, "Rumor has it that the lovers hide behind the walls during the day and come out and waltz together at night." Upstairs, two large oil paintings—one of a woman, the other of a mam—hang above two chairs. She once sat in one of the chairs but "felt so eerie and strange that I never did it again," she said. One day, workers arrived to find both portraits lying on the floor. There was no damage to either, and it seemed as if they had been gently removed. Perhaps Katherine and Michael spend the day within their paintings.

Before bartenders leave for the night, they turn every bottle so the labels face out. Every now and then in the morning, each bottle is found reversed, the labels facing inward. One bartender finished washing each glass and hanging them above the bar. He turned away for less than ten seconds and found each glass upright on the surface of the bar. Chairs placed on top of tables in the evening are found on the floor in the morning.

One morning at 4:00 a.m., the manager was rudely awakened by the alarm company. Door and window sensors were quiet, but internal motion sensors had sounded. The man dutifully investigated, finding all the exterior entrances and windows securely locked before he searched the interior. He found no one and the restaurant in the condition it was in when he left for the night. However, the kitchen was a mess, with pots and pans scattered across the floor and many glass items shattered.

Mary-Alison's most frightening story involved a child. A woman brought her five-year-old daughter while she reserved the piano bar for a Christmas party. Finished with her business, the lady called her girl, who was playing in a corner. Her refusal to leave annoyed the mom, who repeated her instruction. The girl still demurred, saying that "she wanted to play with the soldier," Mary-Alison said. There was no soldier in sight, but the girl described the uniform in such detail that the woman knew it had been a Confederate soldier, perhaps a counterpart of Michael. The mother went home and found photographs of Civil War soldiers online. When an image of a Confederate was accessed, the girl announced that that was the uniform her new friend had been wearing. Mary-Alison found the story scary. "How could the kid know what a uniform looked like? She was five."

One morning, Dianna Avena wrote, after letting himself in and locking the exterior door behind him, a cook saw a woman walk past from the direction of the bathroom. A search revealed no one. On several occasions, as the cook started to unlock the restaurant, at a point near the restrooms, he had been stopped by a knocking on the door from the inside. He wisely waited until other employees arrived before entering.

Workers avoided the upstairs as much as possible. Some swore they had heard Katherine's body swaying from one beam, and they pointed out a gouge carved by the rope on the timber. Considerable activity occurred on the stairs, where sounds like a long dress rustling over the steps was heard.

Sometimes the grand piano upstairs seemed to play itself. The music ceased as hardy investigators appeared, and they always found the piano keys covered.

A writer for *Tables* magazine spoke to bartender Ric Parrish, who had an intimate encounter with a ghostly phenomenon one night after closing as he carried the cash drawer to the office on the second floor.

"There was a mist, like the one from the bottle on *I Dream of Jeannie*," Parrish said, "just hovering in front of a portrait of a 19th century gentleman. I circled the mist and looked at it from all sides. It moved right by me back toward the portrait, and a chill ran up my spine. Then it just disappeared. I dropped the cash drawer and ran."

Another employee told the reporter of an incident that occurred during a thunderstorm. On the landing of the second floor, he observed a couple, dressed in nineteenth-century clothing, dancing gaily.

Ghost Stories of Georgia includes a Public House tale. Atlantan Georgia Schmit was dining with her sister, a resident of Roswell, in the Public House. Concluding their meal, they retired to the piano bar for cognac. The room was empty that Tuesday evening, but they both heard two sets of footsteps across the room. Deciding that the light step was a woman and the heavier tread a man, they first believed the pair were employees cleaning. When the women heard soft whispers, they wondered if the couple was not up to some hanky-panky. Describing the activity to the hostess, they were told that no one could have entered or left the room without being seen. The employee then related the story of the ghost couple.

For two hours on October 8, 2005, seven members of Historic Ghost Watch investigated the Public House. They split into two teams with a one-person base, according to the investigative report posted on their website. The researchers encountered "a great deal of activity," including many "EVPs throughout the restaurant" and "a significant amount of electromagnetic activity." These results led to the belief "that the building is paranormally active." EMF readings were high when Michelle Lowe, one of the investigators and a sensitive, felt something tug on her dress at the bar and when a sound was heard in the ceiling above the piano. Michelle and another team member, David, chased "something" by following EMF readings, which regularly disappeared and reappeared several steps later. Michelle felt a "presence" mounting the stairs and "hanging out" on the top landing and saw a shadow above a camera. She also experienced an "iridescent spider web" that flew past her. Both teams heard a loud noise in the back room, one group reporting that it sounded like "something being dragged across the floor," while the other thought it resembled "moving furniture." A motion detector went off several times. Among the EVPs was, "Who's dead?"

Lowe was lunching with her employer, a doctor, and a drug representative at J. Christopher's. Venturing upstairs, "a cool air came and circled around me" and the doctor and then "actually followed us back to our table," she told Avena. On another occasion, Lowe, the doctor and two others were exiting the restaurant when an upstairs blind "started slamming the window extremely hard," without human assistance.

A Confederate spirit caused a manager to instantly quit. During a busy Sunday, she slumped into a large wing chair upstairs and closed her eyes for a moment. Hearing someone sitting down in an adjacent chair, she opened her eyes. An impression was forming in the cushion, but for a moment, no one was visible. When a Confederate started "to materialize, his face looking directly at her," the woman ran screaming out of the restaurant—permanently. Presumably, Michael and this Confederate have found a way to coexist.

Why so many ghosts are attracted to the bathroom is a continuing mystery. An elderly woman, clad all in white, is seen sitting at the vanity, apparently checking her makeup and hair. As patrons peer into the mirror, the lady in white will appear behind them in the reflection. Whirling around they find no corporeal being. Sometimes when the ladies' room is unoccupied, the toilets flush, water runs in the sink and the door refuses to open.

When J. Christopher's is opened each day, various lights have been out—they have not blown, but are found instead to have been partially unscrewed during the night.

Assistant manager Kristina Paulson has had a number of experiences in the restaurant's kitchen. According to Corinna Underwood in *Haunted History: Atlanta and North Georgia*, Paulson has been touched by unseen beings, and once when she dropped a dish into a sink, the plate hovered briefly before succumbing to gravity and falling normally. At the sink on another occasion, "I felt fingers running from my neck down my spine," she said. She has also felt an invisible being lean over her shoulder and has been pulled backward. Paulson had a sighting of Michael, a shadow man walking through the kitchen at 3:00 a.m.

A kitchen worker was privileged to witness Catherine stroll past him. She did not return his greeting, and disappeared through the wall.

Public House manager Carlton Green commented, "Some customers claim to have seen the Union soldier, but that's usually after a two-hour wait and too many cocktails."

An addition to the complex in 1901, the Roswell Bank, attended to the mill's financial affairs. In 1973, wrote Avena, Richard S. Myrick, president of Historic Roswell, purchased the addition. During the renovation, he discovered $600,999 in Confederate money and $500,000 in Confederate bonds, probably payment by the Confederate government to the Roswell Manufacturing Company for uniforms and other cloth products. The spirit of a Confederate figure has frequently been seen in the building.

The Bulloch House

In 1838, James and Martha Bulloch left the coast for Roswell with six children and six slaves. They bought a ten-acre lot and secured a noted architect, Willis Ball of Connecticut, who produced what is considered to be one of the South's best examples of authentic temple-style Greek Revival. Timber was felled on the property and aged. The structure, made of heart of pine, has two fifty-four-foot beams in the attic. The wood was hand sawed and fastened with wooden pegs and hand-forged nails. Slaves dug local clay and fired all the bricks. This became the home of Theodore Roosevelt's mother.

During the Civil War, two family members served in the Confederate navy, while another worked for the Union army. The Bullock women found themselves exiled in Connecticut. They sent care packages of soap, clothing and necessities to Southern acquaintances and collected money to benefit Confederate prisoners held in the North.

After Sherman's arrival in Roswell, Union cavalry camped on the grounds and certainly made use of the structure itself.

The ghost of Bulloch Hall is related to an eighteenth-century event involving a fourteen-year-old slave girl who fell into a well behind the house and died. She has frequently been heard crying, often from the well, and making attic and porch lights turn on and off. It is said that she was in charge of candles and lanterns in the house, and today, candles not only blow themselves out but also occasionally light spontaneously while at other times they cannot be extinguished. Employees say rocking chairs on the porch move when there is no wind, even speeding up and slowing down, and window curtains sway.

Two ghost tour operators, Joe and Dianna Avena, went out to eat with neighbors and then set out to explore Bullock Hall. At the structure, the neighbor woman felt uncomfortable, so she and Dianna sat in the car while the men scouted the grounds. As they approached the porch, the women saw the curtains in a second-floor window start to shake violently, as if they had been seized by two hands and been vigorously pulled back and forth. When the four drove away, the lights instantly turned off. Later inquiry revealed that the exterior lights were on a timer, which turned them on at dusk and off at dawn. The lights were not motion activated.

Hauntedgeorgia spent a night investigating haunted locales around Roswell. Members were particularly interested in Bulloch Hall, where they saw the flickering lights in the attic and on the porch, and on video, they captured "a weird shadowy figure" that ran in front of a tree "VERY QUICKLY" just one second after the porch lights extinguished themselves. The investigators also captured an EVP, a rattle, heard twice "very loud, very clear." One participant said it "sounded like a door closing and rattling."

The team continued to the Old Roswell Mill Ruins, dating partially from the Civil War, where a picture showed "a man wearing Civil War era clothing and a hat" standing near the mill. There are reports that at night the screams of women, reportedly those torn from family and home, can be heard, as well as the sounds of mill machinery.

Atlanta

High Tech Meets Civil War Spirits

In June 1998, WSB-TV moved into a brand-new, state-of-the-art, $50-million studio in Atlanta, but it seemed that a 140-year old Civil War spirit from the old building also decided to make the transition. The spook spent most of its time in the accounting department, according to one employee. "He lives back there," the man told the *Atlanta Journal Constitution* in November 1998. "The noises come from empty spaces. There is this feeling someone is here. Then you hear things. Things moving. That's why we keep that door closed."

"One night there was nobody here," reported Florence Hatcher in human resources. "I heard furniture rolling across the floor, papers shuffling. He was here."

A third employee, sales executive Eve Whitaker, was alone one night when "something came up behind me and flipped my hair, playfully. I turned around and there was nothing, only this feeling of a presence." Others have reported extremely cold spots and heard the sound of an old-fashioned tin cup sliding across an unoccupied desk.

The communications company called in Cheri Mohr Drake, leader of the Georgia Haunt Hunt Club. She and her associates arrived armed with electromagnetic and thermal sensors. When the instruments indicated an anomaly, the researchers took photographs of the area. Several photos exhibited strange images that had not been obvious to human observers. Orbs of light can be an indication of spirit activity, but the photos also displayed a unique streak of green light and a faint face in a window, peaking over blinds.

Orbs were found around a desk frequented by the ghost, where the green streak was also recorded, and on walls and ceilings and outside the facility.

Employees refer to the soldier as the General, said Hatcher. "He looks like a private in the pictures, but we promoted him to general. It never hurts to be on the good side of a ghost."

"You look and say, 'That's something,'" said executive producer Susan Stone. "It has on one of those Civil War caps. You know, you have a powerful reason to believe in something like that."

"He must have been aroused by something," said accounting secretary Jamie Pope.

So why has this Civil War soldier haunted a space age facility? "We were built on the Confederate trenches," said Hatcher. "Our thinking is, he was disturbed with all the digging that was going on."

The WSB operations manager challenged this statement. "We didn't see any signs of trenches," he said. "We told everyone if they found anything to let me know and nobody did."

To settle the dispute, the late Franklin Garrett, Atlanta's premier historian for many decades, declared that the site lies in the center of Southern lines. A nearby historical marker supports this finding. Confederate troops left the protection of these fortifications to attack Union forces crossing Peachtree Creek. In that battle, a Confederate defeat, 2,500 Southern and 1,900 Northern troops fell.

Soon after it opened, the new WSB building was criticized by Catherine Fox, the *Atlanta Journal Constitution* visual arts critic. She noted that a pyramid on the roof glowed at night and made "it look more like an alien spaceship than the headquarters of a major company."

Peachtree Creek

As Sherman crossed the Chattahoochee River, Confederate president Jefferson Davis removed Johnston from command and replaced him with John Hood. The new commander attempted to strike the Federals as they crossed Peachtree Creek, but the Southerners were decimated.

An Internet posting by LBG897 in 2001 claimed that if you walk along Peachtree Creek in the early evening, "you feel the presence of Civil War ghosts." That is the only indication of local paranormal activity, for upscale neighborhoods tend to keep their haunts to themselves.

Foxy Ghosts

Although it is not antebellum, Atlanta's Fox Theater is one of the city's oldest preserved and restored properties. Started in the 1920s as a gaudy Masonic lodge, the building was soon a grand movie palace and venue for live entertainment. During the Civil War, the site was occupied by a Confederate fortification labeled *K*. Gizgremlin reported that his mother, a Fox employee during the late 1940s and through the '50s, "used to tell us about the secret passages there, and a lot of weird stuff that would happen

The Battle of Peachtree Creek has produced few ghosts, but they prowl beside the stream at night near old mill remains.

when no one was there. She told me she saw the Confederate drummer boy there several times." Somehow these tunnels have become associated with the storage of munitions during the Civil War and a uniformed guard has reportedly been sighted. Stories also circulate that the face of a Confederate enlisted man has been observed in windows. Many patrons and employees have been startled by the sight.

Reacting to stories such as these, Ghost Hounds conducted a nighttime investigation on July 20, 2006. Denisee reported that the team was allowed "into every nook and cranny" and "witnessed several anomalies," including "an FBA [full body apparition] in the ladies' restroom." Hoot-n-toot related, "We did experience major battery drain in certain areas, and a female energy was felt very strongly by me where Denisee saw the FBA. All the hair on my body was standing up during the experience!" This electrical charge, she later added, made her feel "a big bubble of electrical energy surrounding me. What was a first for me is that I could actually feel how far around me this energy field was. It was two or more feet beyond my body in every direction around me. It was very intense and then after a few seconds it suddenly disappeared."

Oakland Cemetery: A Bivouac of the Dead

The monotonous rows of soldier's graves at Oakland Cemetery stretch longer every day.
—*Scarlet O'Hara,* Gone With the Wind

"The Bivouac of the Dead," by Theodore O'Hara, was written to honor the dead of the Mexican American War and became a popular addition to Civil War memorials.

The muffled drum's sad roll has beat
The soldier's last tattoo!
No more on life's parade shall meet
The brave and fallen few.
On Fame's eternal camping ground
Their silent tents are spread,
And Glory guards with solemn round
The bivouac of the dead.

The Confederate dead of Oakland Cemetery are guarded by this magnificent stone lion. At dusk some have heard a roll call of the dead.

If any site in Atlanta deserves to be haunted it would be Oakland Cemetery. The City of Atlanta purchased the land in 1850, and an estimated forty-five thousand people are buried there, including author Margaret Mitchell—whose ghost has been reported—golfer Bobby Jones, five Georgia governors, twenty-three Atlanta mayors, five Confederate generals and thousands of Confederate soldiers. Captain Benjamin H. Helm, Abraham Lincoln's brother-in-law, was wounded at Chickamauga but died in an Atlanta hospital, and he was temporarily buried there. In the postwar period, Confederate vice-president Alexander Stephens was initially interred there after a funeral attended by twenty thousand people.

No rumor of the foe's advance
Now swells upon the wind,
Nor troubles thought of midnight haunts,
Of loved ones left behind;
No vision of the morrow's strife
The warrior's dream alarms,
No braying horn or screaming fife
A dawn to call to arms.

Up to four thousand unidentified Confederate dead lie beneath neatly ordered rows of tombstones, many reinterred from area battlefields following the war or casualties from Atlanta's many hospitals, all gathered there in 1872. Towering above them and honoring their memory is a tall stone obelisk dedicated a year later.

Adjacent to the Confederate plot is one of the most moving memorials in the nation. In 1894 the Lion of Atlanta was revealed. The thirty-thousand-pound monument, carved from a single block of Georgia marble, depicts a courageous lion dying of wounds, mournfully clasping a Confederate flag.

Their shivered swords are red with rust,
Their plume'd heads are bowed,
Their haughty banner, trailed in dust,
Is now their martial shroud—
And plenteous funeral tears have washed
The red stains from each brow,
And the proud forms by battle gashed
Are free from anguish now.

I'M A CEMETERY COP, I WEAR A BADGE

A number of writers have made the following story their own, but I have tracked down its origin, an issue of *American Weekly* magazine published in the fall of 1933 and popularized by John P. Bessor in the article "Restless Spirits," published in the March 1953 issue of *FATE* magazine.

According to the original accounts, paranormal activity at Oakland Cemetery was first manifested in 1933. Ghostly figures flitting among the tombs and gravestones, a spectral roll call of soldiers buried in Oakland and the tolling of the sexton's bell were all reported incidents to the Atlanta Police Department. Authorities responded by assigning a series of officers to patrol the cemetery, but none lasted long.

E.H. Bentley, a veteran policeman, had the first tour. Each night, he locked the heavy iron entrance gates, but still the sexton's big bell rang nightly, even after he climbed into the belfry and disconnected the rope. Nor was there sufficient wind to shake the bell. After a few nights, Bentley asked for a transfer, claiming, "I'll go stark mad if I'm not."

Bentley was replaced by a volunteer, John Rumph, who reported seeing beautiful mermaids and hearing their laughter as they frolicked in a memorial

One cemetery cop believed the sexton's house at Oakland was the center of paranormal activity. He was wrong—it was everywhere.

fountain in the moonlight. He died soon thereafter, following commitment to Georgia's insane asylum in Milledgeville.

Graveyard Shift

The third policeman sent on the graveyard beat was World War I veteran Ed Cason, who cruised the cemetery lanes on a bicycle. As he pedaled one night, he suddenly became aware of a ghostly figure keeping pace to one side. In terror, Officer Ed pedaled harder, but he became disoriented and crashed into the locked gates. Knocked out for hours, the spook at least was gone when he awakened. Cason was relieved of this horrific duty but was left with a permanent scar across his forehead.

The Atlanta Police Department next turned to "one of the biggest, most fearless policeman on the force," W.H. Swords. He determined that the paranormal activity emanated from the sexton's office and stationed himself there. As soon as Swords entered, he could feel the presence of many unseen spirits and then heard whispering that he could not understand. The brave officer cut off the lights and immediately heard a knock on the back door. He quickly moved to the door and silently grasped the knob. At the next rap, he threw the door open, but nothing was there. Swords repeated this effort three more times before shifting his attention outside, where he secreted himself behind a tombstone to watch the backdoor of the sexton's office. He did not sight the prankster he suspected responsible for the knocking but said, "Then I simply froze in my tracks. From right beside me came the soft notes of a bugle. In a moment I heard the throaty voice of an unseen man who seemed to be calling the roll of the dead. 'Jack Smith?' the voice intoned and from a little distance away came the answer, 'Here!'"

As Swords swept his flashlight across the sea of gravestones, he saw nothing, but he did hear the continuing roll call of the dead. He soon secured other work.

The ordinary soldiers buried at Oakland may be unknown to the living, but they are known to each other, there on the last campground, the bivouac of the dead.

"I saw a ghost and shot at it," said the next cemetery patrolman. "I couldn't have missed it but there is nothing there now." Those words were spoken to Officer W.H. Dobb, who was driving an Atlanta patrol wagon past the cemetery when the shots were fired. Dobb immediately stopped to assist his colleague, leaping the fence to find him holding his smoking gun, wild-eyed and trembling. The officer was relieved of this spooky duty.

THE CRYPT KEEPER

A final officer had the most startling vision at Oakland Cemetery. The frightened policeman exited the cemetery one morning to report that he had seen the ghost of Confederate general John B. Gordon, who actually surrendered Confederate troops at Appomattox and was an outstanding military commander, governor and U.S. senator. He now rests at Oakland. The general was in his full glory, astride a white steed, waving his sword and issuing quiet orders to his staff, which stood attentively nearby.

The neighing troop, the flashing blade,
The bugle's stirring blast,
The charge, the dreadful cannonade,
The din and shout, are passed;
Nor war's wild notes, nor glory's peal
Shall thrill with fierce delight
Those breasts that nevermore shall feel
The rapture of the fight.

Like the fierce Northern hurricane
That sweeps the great plateau,
Flushed with the triumph yet to gain,
Come down the serried foe,
Who heard the thunder of the fray
Break o'ver the field beneath,
Knew the watchword of the day
Was 'Victory or death!'

If all the names of the dead are spoken, then this is indeed a long roll call. One wonders if they also call the names of Union dead inadvertently buried here.

Note that a number of writers have made this classic story their own, personalizing the details and adding variations. Accept no substitutes.

Rest on, embalmed and sainted dead,
Dear is the blood you gave—
No impious footstep here shall tread
The herbage of your grave.
Nor shall your glory be forgot

While Fame her record keeps,
Or honor points the hallowed spot
Where valor proudly sleeps.

Oakland has other important Civil War associations. In July 1864, John Hood observed the Battle of Atlanta from the grounds, which provide a sweeping view of the modern city. Earlier, in June 1862, six of the men who stole the engine General in the Great Locomotive Chase were hanged here and buried on the grounds before reinterment at the Chattanooga National Cemetery

In June 1998, the Georgia Haunt Hunt Club descended on Oakland Cemetery, finding swirling mists and orbs in the visitors' center.

Jackie Behrend, in *Ghosts of America's East Coast*, relates two Oakland Cemetery war stories that have come to her attention, one involving a Confederate, the other a Federal.

BLINDED BY THE SIGHT

Blair Underwood entered the cemetery one day to lay flowers on her grandfather's grave and pray. Hurried by a threatening storm, Underwood turned to leave and saw a man lying on the ground who was apparently asleep. The young man walked quietly across the grounds, trying not to disturb the figure, but closer, he "saw blood literally pouring out of his chest." Realizing the wound might prove fatal, Underwood ran toward the man to offer assistance. Suddenly, his eyes popped open, and his head turned toward Underwood, revealing not eyes but empty hollows: "He had no eyes!" The prostrate figure turned away from Underwood and disappeared. Underwood declared this the most horrible sight of his life. Reflecting on the time of the incident, Underwood shuddered to think what might happen at Oakland at night.

SUSPENDED IN TIME AND SPACE

The other incident also occurred in the bright light of day and a century earlier. The account came from an anonymous source, a common occurrence for ghost researchers. An elderly woman showed Behrend a letter her great-grandmother wrote to her grandmother in 1891. The account related what she called a "vision, so disturbing" she could not get it out of her mind and would only tell her daughter lest people "believe me insane." After laying a wreath on the grave of her uncle Andrew, "I witnessed a man hanging from a tree." The figure was wearing "the style of the war," and she believed he was a "Yankee." She looked away from the terrible sight and spent several minutes composing herself. Finally looking up, the spirit had vanished. This is our first spectral reenactment of the Raider's executions.

At the end of a workday, Devin Kuharic, a gardener at Oakland, was starting his car when it quickly honked its own horn four times. That had never occurred before, nor did it ever occur afterward. Years later, driving a new car, Kuharic gave a friend a tour, and as he started the vehicle to leave, "the horn in *that* car honked four times by itself," he told William Bender. Again, such a thing never occurred again.

Yon marble minstrel's voiceless stone
In deathless song shall tell,
When many a vanquished year hath flown,
The story how you fell.
Nor wreck nor change, nor winter's blight,
Nor time's remorseless doom,
Can dim one ray of holy light
That gilds your glorious tomb.

A Confederate Grant and Margaret Mitchell

In 1840, engineer Lemuel P. Grant arrived from Maine to build railroads. He made a fortune and purchased a great deal of land (1,200 acres) in southeast Atlanta, where in 1857, he constructed a huge Italianate mansion with 8,250 square feet and nine fireplaces. As a Confederate colonel, Grant constructed the extensive fortifications that surrounded Atlanta, works so strong that Sherman refused to assault them. The Grant house was used as a military hospital and then spared Sherman's torch, reportedly because of Masonic materials found inside.

Postwar, Grant donated one hundred acres of Grant Park and sold the land to be used for Grady Hospital. After his wife died, he remarried and moved in 1882. In 1902, famed golfer Bobby Jones was born there.

The house changed hands seven times within a few years and became dilapidated, but in 1941, Margaret Mitchell was convinced to loan newspaperman Boyd Taylor $3,500 to restore the mansion. Unfortunately, Taylor became a mysterious hermit. Repeated fires destroyed the roof, and the upper floors collapsed, leaving only thick brick walls.

The weirdness at the Grant mansion started with Taylor. Mitchell, who was concerned about the destruction or division of such buildings into apartments, sued Taylor for breach of contract when she discovered he had demolished the structure's original porches. She won a temporary injunction barring further work, but the case was lost in 1948. Mitchell was killed a year later, after being hit by an off-duty taxi driver on Peachtree Street.

The eccentric Taylor remained in the house for thirty additional years. He camped in the midst of the ruins without electricity or running water, a shotgun by his side and German shepherds roaming the grounds, which were enclosed by a tall chain link fence.

In 1979, Taylor told an *Atlanta Journal Constitution* reporter that each spring, the ghost of Margaret Mitchell visited him bearing flowers from her grave in Oakland Cemetery. "I know no one will believe that she really comes here now, but she does—every spring. I can only tell you what I see. And I can only tell you not to be afraid of ghosts. Margaret just wanders through the house looking things over," he said. "She never talks. And she always carries jonquils. The first night she came, I was very shocked. I went out to her grave in Oakland Cemetery the next day. I'd never been there before. But I was almost certain of what I'd find. The plot is covered by a bed of jonquils." Apparently, Mitchell had forgiven Taylor for his sacrilege. When Taylor died in 1981, police officers were forced to shoot several of his dogs in order to reach the body.

Interior designer Woodrow Mankin purchased the house in 1994 and had friends over for a "cleansing ritual," actually an exorcism of the property. Afterward, a psychic told Mankin that a huge, gold-framed, cloudy mirror, dating to 1854 and one of the few original furnishings from the Grant house present in the living quarters he fashioned within the ruins, was cursed. He covered it with black cloth. He soon died of heart failure at age thirty-seven. Mankin's remains were cremated, and mourners at a memorial service were requested to scatter handfuls of ashes about the grounds.

According to Jim Auchmutey, an *Atlanta Journal Constitution* reporter, the next owner told a neighbor, "I'm superstitious. They didn't put any ashes inside the house, did they?" However, things have turned around for the grand Grant mansion. In 2001, the Atlanta Preservation Center purchased the Grant House at 327 St. Paul Avenue Southeast and restored it as offices for its organization. It is one of only six antebellum structures remaining in Atlanta.

Confessions of a Scientist

John Downey, of St. Joseph County, Michigan, had wanted to join the Eleventh Michigan Volunteers when it marched off to war in 1861, but he had to wait until he turned eighteen several years later. He enlisted to serve with his neighbors in the Eleventh before the trenches of Atlanta in August 1864. On August 7, the Eleventh was ordered to attack the well-fortified Confederate line, which consisted of two positions—one fortification at the edge of a forest, the second farther into the woods. The Eleventh Michigan was to seize the first line, but having accomplished that mission, some continued into the woods. The second assault was crushed, and seven men were reported missing. Among those were Daniel Baldwin—Downey's best friend—George Quay and George W. Lockwood.

During the night, the Federals reversed the exterior ditch of the work they had occupied and withdrew behind their lines on August 10. At breakfast the next day, the regiment was horrified when Lockwood staggered into camp, having suffered multiple wounds.

"His eyes were sunken far back in his head," Downey wrote decades later, "his cheeks were hollow, the ghastly pallor of death was upon his face, and he was so weak that he reeled and staggered as he walked. A dead man from the grave could not have startled us more."

The horror multiplied that night when Downey's friend Baldwin also entered camp. Spying Downey, Baldwin placed a finger across his lips to silence his comrade and gestured for him to follow. The bright moon revealed that Baldwin was also in bad shape, but Downey assumed he was being led to Quay or the other soldiers still missing in action.

At the fortification they had reversed, Baldwin made an effort to speak but issued no sound. He continued into the woods. Downey twice demanded an explanation, and when he refused to continue, Baldwin reproached him with a look. The two walked forward into the dark forest. Eventually, Baldwin turned to Downey, opened his blouse to show "a great blotch of blood" over his heart and pointed toward tall weeds along a stream. At that point, Baldwin faded away.

"Cold with terror," Downey raced to camp and awoke his friend Tim. Explaining what had happened, they returned and found two decomposing bodies. In the morning, a stretcher detail retrieved the bloated corpses, and a search of their clothing proved them to be the bodies of Baldwin and Quay. Downey required Tim to swear he would never recount the tale.

The regiment soon mustered out, arriving home on September 25, 1864. Downey attended university, became a distinguished teacher in Pennsylvania, dean of the College of Science, Literature and the Arts at the University of Minnesota and a math professor in China at the Universities of Nanking and Peking. He authored a number of noted works on math and science.

Thirty years after the war, Downey finally wrote an account of his paranormal experience at Atlanta. As he was "unwilling" to attribute it to a "supernatural agency," Downey attempted to find a scientific explanation. He was never successful in that quest.

That is one of the most substantial Civil War ghost stories I have ever encountered. It appeared in the August 2003 issue of *FATE* magazine, authored by Daniel J. Wood, an academic living in St. Joseph County, Michigan.

A General's Ghost

Union major general James B. McPherson was only thirty-five years old when he arrived with Sherman to attack Atlanta. His rise in rank had been rapid, and he now commanded the Army of the Tennessee, a unit led before him by U.S. Grant as well as Sherman. The commanding general had much faith in and affection for the young general. McPherson had asked for leave so he could marry his fiancée, but Sherman declared that would have to wait until this campaign was over.

On July 22, 1864, Confederate troops savagely attacked the Army of the Tennessee as it closed in on Atlanta. The surprise assault caught McPherson away from his command, and he spurred his horse forward in hopes of regaining control of a perilous situation. Inadvertently, McPherson rode straight into a Confederate breakthrough. Seeing enemy troops swarming through the woods, the general reined in his horse and reversed direction. Southerners shouted for McPherson to surrender, but he refused. A volley of rifle fire knocked the young man from his horse, killing him instantly. When McPherson's body was recovered, it was displayed on a door in Sherman's headquarters. The shaken commander was reported to have wept at the sight. His protégé was dead and would never have a family.

General John Logan took command of the Army of the Tennessee and successfully repelled the Confederate attack. Several days later,

Sherman ordered Logan to sweep around Atlanta, from the eastern edge to the western, in an attempt to destroy the railroads that supplied the Confederates. According to William Key's book *The Battle of Atlanta and the Georgia Campaign*, as the army marched through the night toward Ezra Church, a whisper raced through the ranks: McPherson was riding at the head of the column, leading his army into one last battle. That combat, another Union victory, occurred just west of Atlanta University and east of Westview Cemetery, at Ezra Church.

McPherson was killed at the modern intersection of Monument and McPherson, just off Glenwood in east Atlanta, the site marked today by a cannon buried muzzle up.

The Headless Ghost of Underground

Underground Atlanta originated at surface level, where the first mile marker on the Western & Atlantic Railroad was established in 1838. When the Georgia Railroad Freight Depot was constructed in 1869, the passage of one hundred trains arriving and departing daily made it far too dangerous to cross the street at this busy Union Street location. A number of iron bridges were built crossing above the railroad, extending from the second floor of buildings on either side of the tracks. This became the basis of a second floor of concrete bridges with a plaza and parks and retail establishments. A third level was added later, and the second layer became the Underground. Most of Atlanta's visitors and even residents are unaware of the first floor, located on the actual ground, used by businesses for servicing and storage.

According to William Bender, for years security and maintenance personnel have seen a figure clad in a Confederate uniform—sometimes headless, other times with head intact—late at night walking the tracks. It is always late at night, with few witnesses around, and the ghost never notices or interacts with the living. Although his rank has never been established, the spirit has been dubbed "Colonel C.J."

As to his origins, I am reminded of one of the most intense scenes in *Gone with the Wind*—Scarlett staring helplessly at the mass of wounded soldiers that occupied the corner of Pryor and Alabama Streets.

An Andersonville Ghost at Anthony's Restaurant

Anthony's Restaurant (3109 Piedmont Road Northeast) started its existence in Washington, Georgia, in 1797, as the Pope-Walton House, located on a 2,500-acre plantation that held hundreds of slaves. With the end of the war, many Confederate troops trudged home from surrendered armies in Virginia and North Carolina. Union occupation saw the home looted but left Mary Elizabeth Pope Walton, the Northern-born daughter of Lula Belle Walton, and wet nurse Sarah Walton safe. In the late 1960s, the house was moved over a three-year period and restored for the restaurant.

Bells heard ringing late at night are attributed to Lula Belle. It was thought that Mary Elizabeth played with the electrical systems, commonly turning lights on and off, and appeared as the Lady in White on the staircase and the upstairs foyer. After carefully turning off the chandelier upstairs, witnesses had stood feet from the switch and heard the chandelier click on. Many also heard the mewing of a phantom cat and felt it brush by under tables and on the staircase.

An odd part of Anthony's was a wooden door to the wine cellar, which had a barred section in the middle, where much ghostly phenomena occurred. The door was an original artifact removed from the notorious Confederate prison camp at Andersonville. Here workers saw the ghost of a young black woman clad in mid-1800s apparel. She has also been seen in other parts of the house going about her business. This was thought to be the spirit of Lucinda Pope, who worked in the house as a slave and as a free employee before dying at the age of twenty-eight in 1870. Anthony's had two wine cellars, and she could be found at both locations.

In 1998, general manager Mary Dean Aguirre gave Alan Levine, a reporter for the *Vinings Gazette* permission to spend a night alone in the restaurant. Aguirre had never seen a ghost, but she refused to stay there alone at night. She referred the reporter to former manager Sallie Cwik, who told him, "Yes, the house is haunted. There's a main staircase at the front of the building. Near there is an old photograph of Annie Barnett who was married in the house in 1882. Some people sense her presence near the staircase; others have heard children singing there. We've even had employees quit after being in the house late at night because they thought it was haunted."

Cwik had never seen a ghost, but one night, she and her husband had just closed the restaurant for the evening, which included unscrewing the bulbs from the upstairs sconces—there was no light switch there. The couple left, only to see from the parking lot that the upstairs lights were blazing away. "Yet when we went back into the house, the bulbs were screwed in tight. So we unscrewed them again and went back to our car in the parking lot. We looked up at the house…and the lights were all back on again!"

Levine chose the autumn equinox, September 22, for his visit. He heard three raps on the ceiling overhead and then bangs, followed by "the sound of bells—high pitched and beautiful like an angel song."

After Levine lay in his sleeping bag on the floor before the stairs, the terror started:

> *Then I heard the sound of footsteps, soft but distinct and coming up the stairs. And rustling too. I huddled down deeper into my sleeping bag. The footsteps arrived at the top of the stairs and began to walk towards me. I poke my head out to see who was there. But nothing. Only the feeling of another presence. And the rustling. Someone invisible was just a few feet from me. I couldn't speak. My voice was gone. There we stayed for an uncountable duration. Me and my host. The presence slowly faded. I tried to relax. The soft footsteps and rustling began again. From the bottom of the stairs, up and to me, the presence came. And again I stared hard down the hall searching, but saw no one. Three times the presence came up the stairs but never went down.*

Finally, Levine slept.

After the living returned to the restaurant in the morning, Levine called his wife on their anniversary. "I had a strange dream last night," she told him. "We were together at Anthony's. A woman I've never seen before in a dress unlike anything you'd see today brought me to you."

In 2003, Patrick Burns led a team from Ghost Hounds to Anthony's. When Burns asked a deceased resident to "give us a sign," an overhead track light turned itself on, according to Alan Brown in *Haunted Georgia*. Soon, investigator Christine "came running out of the women's room with her pants around her ankles." Christine explained that the toilet paper roll started spinning as if a cat were playing with it. Burns sat near the stall in a chair and almost immediately he heard "dudududududu!" Opening the stall, he found several feet of toilet paper strewn across the floor. When Burns returned a year later, he found the level of activity to be "staggering. The cameraman went running down the stairs. He said something reached out and touched him," something invisible

"Patrons occasionally see a woman dressed in antebellum clothing," said Cheri Drake, who investigated the restaurant. One of her photos captured an orb at the place where the ghost is usually sighted, and a picture taken of the outside staircase showed the fuzzy outline of a ghost cat on the top stair. A bright orb appeared on a photo of the management office, on the floor where a worker died while working late.

Unfortunately, Anthony's Restaurant has closed.

Supernatural Restoration

Meadownook (Alston Drive at East Lake Country Club, 1856), a coastal planter–style home with Greek Revival details, was constructed by Colonel Robert Alston as a wedding present for his wife. While Alston was stationed during the war at Charleston, his wife and children remained there, and Union and Confederate generals occupied the structure. It is said that soldiers were rallied during the Battle of Atlanta by slamming rifles on a rail of the staircase, which is still marred. One story has a Union soldier killed by a Confederate sharpshooter during the battle. In the yard is the headstone of George M. Rikard, an Alabama cavalryman mortally wounded by an exploding artillery shell on July 22. He died hours later and a letter to his wife revealed that he was buried in the southwest corner of the garden. In 2001, 137 years late, one hundred descendants of Rikard gathered in the garden for the placement of a marker near a gazebo. President Jefferson Davis, Alexander Stephens and John B. Gordon visited the house.

Colonel Alston returned home to manage his four-hundred-acre plantation and represent DeKalb County in the general assembly, where he fought Georgia's brutal convict labor system until assassinated in 1878. He is buried in the Decatur Cemetery.

The Alston house was unoccupied for years, then spent decades as a rental unit, usually inhabited by college students. In the 1970s, while a group of Georgia Tech students were in residence, all but one had left to eat. The lone student was studying intently when a sock dropped on his back. He was annoyed with his housemates until he realized that he was alone in the house. Another party of renters broke their lease and moved out rather than occupy the haunted house.

In 1994, a nurse and her big dog occupied the structure. While she slept upstairs, the dog kept watch downstairs. Two times sounds like breaking dishes downstairs so spooked the animal that it bounded up the stairs, loosed its bowels in fear and leaped into the bed. The pair soon moved out.

Sylvia and Charles Harrison purchased the historic structure in 1994 and then spent two years renovating. The restored home has won a preservation award from the Atlanta Urban Design Commission. It has thirteen-foot ceilings, a fancy curving staircase, marble mantels, floor-length windows and hardwood floors. The colonel's desk and an antique organ remain. The odd point here is that much of the restoration seems to have originated with the home's builder, Colonel Alston, dead over a century.

"We just sort of let the house direct us," revealed Sylvia. "We've tried to redo it as Colonel Alston intended it to be. It's nice for us that we like what he did." The restoration, sometimes guided by hunches, has been endorsed by descendants of the Alston family. "The house kind of guided us as to what it needed," Charles said. "I'm not sure that the colonel's ghost hasn't been helping us."

"It's just amazing they were able to do this without any advice from preservationists," said Susan Gwinnard of the Commission. "They knew all the right things to do."

After the restoration was completed, the Harrisons learned that the Alston family had hung a painting of the Madonna over the fireplace in the dining room and placed a walnut settee, upholstered in red, in the parlor. The Harrisons had installed the exact same touches in those identical places.

The house has long been reputed to be haunted, and previous owners told the Harrisons some spooky tales of the home. A photograph taken inside seems to be distorted by a bright light, and some have felt a chill within. Sylvia admitted that the family had experienced several paranormal events in the residence. Charles felt a presence nearby as he sat at the dining room table. Spirits seemed to help Sylvia locate misplaced items, and they have rearranged family pictures, perhaps while studying the faces of the new inhabitants, and placed them facedown or turned the faces to the wall, as if they do not care for them. Pictures and other items are found in the middle of the room. Instead of falling normally off a mantle or table, Sylvia commented, "[they] would project." A common paranormal event has been experienced—the feeling of being surrounded by a spider web—in this house while sitting at the dining room table.

"A few people have said they've felt like they're walking into spider webs," said Sylvia. "My son won't stay in the upstairs bedroom when he visits because he said he feels like somebody's touching his face." The son, temporarily occupying the upstairs bedroom, awoke on his first night to what seemed to him to be a man's weight sitting on his chest and pinning him to the bed. He struggled to turn over, but when he did, the phenomenon was repeated. The son started spending nights on the first floor in a sleeping bag, refusing to venture upstairs again.

While preparing a special birthday dinner one day, Sylvia searched the kitchen for a can of olives before calling Charlie and asking him to stop at the store on his way home. Walking back to the kitchen, Sylvia told William N. Bender in *Haunted Atlanta and Beyond*, a cabinet opened by itself, "and a can rolled out on the floor." The can contained olives. "It gives me chill bumps now," she said. "I just about died."

The house is said to be haunted by the spirits of Colonel Alston and a Union soldier shot in the foyer by a Confederate soldier. Other casualties are thought to have been buried on the grounds. On the other hand, "We've had some people say they felt it was a woman," Sylvia said, "but I like to think it's the colonel. He was a rather handsome fellow."

DeKalb County

Decatur: Civil War Ghosts at the Women's College

During the Battle of Atlanta, war came to the campus of Agnes Scott College (1899) in Decatur. Union troops had circled east of the city to cut the Augusta Railroad. As John Hood attacked James McPherson, Joseph Wheeler's Confederate cavalry attacked the Union wagon train in Decatur. Initially successful, the assault was recalled when Hood's action failed. An engraved stone on the campus indicates the main scene of the battle, and a second stone at the old courthouse records further fighting that day.

Although this spirit has not been glimpsed in decades, the school's most famous ghost is the Blue Lady, according to *Haunted Atlanta and Beyond*. The Blue Lady haunts the upper floors of Presser Hall, which occupies the highest point on campus. In 1864, that spot was occupied by a church, and there is a story that a young woman was tasked with warning the population in general and the Confederate military specifically of approaching enemy forces. However, she was killed before accomplishing her mission, we assume by some dastard Federal. An alternate version has the Blue Lady as a widow searching for her husband, who was killed in the battle.

Another ghost is said to haunt Presser Hall, a trustee who, for some reason, opposed adding an elevator to the structure. The device was installed despite her objections, and she is said to inhabit the elevator, causing it to operate independently of human control, moving between floors of its own accord, much like its sister machinery at the Marietta Museum of History.

Agnes Scott has another ghost, a female art professor, who roams the Dana Fine Arts Building. Killed by an unfortunate accident with a pottery kiln (is anyone else flashing on *Animal House?*) young students often feel uncomfortable working late in the evening.

Stone Mountain

Long before the grand Confederate memorial was carved onto the face of the great granite monolith, Stone Mountain was a village that hosted Confederate hospitals and endured Union cavalry raids on its railroad facilities. The city cemetery hosts a Confederate section of 150 veterans. The Village Inn (1820s), one of the oldest structures in town, has three floors and twelve rooms; the top floor was originally a ballroom. The inn was a Civil War hospital and was a bed-and-breakfast. During the war, the most seriously wounded were treated there, while less critical cases were tended at the nearby square. For those who died, the cemetery was mere blocks away.

During renovations in 1995, wallboards on the second floor were found to have the names of soldiers carved in them. The owner believed the men feared dying unknown and recorded their existence in wood. Undoubtedly, some of the soldiers did succumb to their wounds. One board, carved with the name Sergeant Frank Nash, was preserved and kept in a room downstairs beside a fireplace. Many mornings the board has been found to be relocated. Owner Christie Collins dubbed the ghost Frank Nash. After the engraved boards were found, things began shifting about with greater frequency. Collins witnessed metal foil slide along a kitchen counter and ink pens propelled themselves across a desk.

In 1868, after its wartime service, a local minister converted the building into his home; it remained in the family for 125 years before undergoing a 2-year renovation in 1994–95. While a private home, one owner described a woman who was seen standing at the top of the second-floor stairs. "From her appearance," manager Ashley Anderson told Corinna Underwood in *Haunted History: Atlanta and North Georgia*, "they assumed it was the ghost of one of the former nurses from the time the inn was used as a hospital for Confederate soldiers." Since her tenure began in 2003, "guests have reported seeing a woman in period dress, sitting at a mirrored dresser, removing bobby pins from her hair in one of the bedrooms." Guests have heard the laughter of children, phantom footsteps—both running and walking—soft music playing and other mysterious sounds. There were also reports of moving shadows, shifted belongings, whistling, whispering and, most uniquely, Morse code messages. (As a former Boy Scout, I have to wonder if anyone ever attempted deciphering those ethereal missives.) Ceiling fans turned on, and lights went off by themselves. This is apparently a happy ghost, casually going about his haunting business.

When two sisters, one of whom is a sensitive, visited, the psychic felt the presence of three spirits, who were "here to help and protect you," William N. Benter reported in *Haunted Atlanta and Beyond*. "I can feel them around you, but I feel like they are here to help you and protect you; not to harm you."

According to Reese Christian in *Ghosts of Atlanta*, Scarlett's Room seemed to contain a female ghost, appropriately enough. A hairbrush was seen suspended in space before dropping to the floor. A heavy perfume was detected in the morning, and a wardrobe door opened itself. In Rhett's Room, which contained boards engraved by soldiers, a chair rocked spontaneously. A past owner, sleeping in the room, woke to hear an elderly man singing a spiritual. On the veranda, she heard nothing, but the song continued within the room, seemingly at close range. A young man who appeared in the mirror of the Angel Room spoke silently before fading away.

Inside the Yellow Room, an invisible spirit sat on the bed beside a guest. As a couple was discussing the recent death of an infant daughter, a child's antique dress fell from a shadow box.

The longtime housekeeper refused to enter the Blue Room alone because it harbored a presence. Collins kept her on for a while, but the woman quit in fear after, she said, a ghost followed her up and down the stairs. At one time, a woman descending those stairs spotted a flash of light before she had an "overwhelming feeling that she was not supposed to look up at that exact moment."

In April 1997, a couple who had rented the whole facility for their wedding bedded down in the Blue Room. At 3:30 a.m., the door flew open and slammed against the wall. Both felt a "presence" in the room.

One Halloween night, a couple called the owner to report that their room was freezing and wasps were buzzing about. Another couple later complained of the extreme cold.

The owner once left the Village Inn for her home next door and glanced up at the ballroom, illuminated by lights, and saw figures walk past the window. She knew there was no one in the ballroom. From that large room the sounds of children, music and parties were heard.

In the Village Inn objects moved of their own accord, and items propped up against a wall fell over. People felt watched, and equipment was seemingly teleported to other rooms. Doors opened and closed, lights turned on and off, the odor of pipe smoke was detected, and candles were knocked into bathtubs. Chains on room doors rattled.

The Wanderers in Tucker

An interesting Internet posting from a Georgia man related an experience in a girlfriend's house in Tucker some years past. The couple was conversing on a couch in a sunken living room when they heard someone descending the stairs toward them. The man noted that the girl was grinning as he turned to identity the visitor. There was no one to be seen; but the footsteps were clearly audible, and a weight was visibly being applied to each stair in succession. When the presence turned into the garage, the man followed. He sensed something to his right and turned, but he still saw nothing. He then felt that "it" had passed through the wall.

A number of skirmishes were fought in the area during the Civil War, and research revealed a trench line that cut through the neighborhood. The young woman revealed that friends along her street, living in a series of houses constructed in a straight line, had similar experiences. At least the walkabout spirit was considerate enough to shut all the doors it opened.

Clayton County

Jonesboro

Spirits Prefer the Way Things Were

After fighting three major battles for Atlanta and maintaining a two-month siege, Sherman devised his final tactic. The Federal army circled far to the southwest and struck Atlanta's last railroad supply lines near Jonesboro. Hood's Confederates were forced to attack, which resulted in a significant Union victory and possession of Atlanta.

The Warren House, a three-story house occupying a hill overlooking the railroad depot in Jonesboro, was constructed in 1860 by Guy L. Warren,

The Warren House in Jonesboro is one of Georgia's most haunted buildings. Occupants have seen a number of Civil War soldiers in the building.

an agent for the Macon and Western Railroad and one of the town's first commissioners. Much of the fiercest fighting in the two-day battle fought there in the summer of 1864 occurred in that area. Federal surgeons commandeered the house for use as a field hospital, performing countless operations in an upstairs room. One third-story room is still known as the "death room," where hopeless cases were left to die.

Over the past 135 years, the Warren House attained a reputation for being haunted. In the mid-1980s, the house underwent a two-year renovation in preparation for its use as corporate headquarters for American Home Health Care. Timothy DeCapria did much of the construction. At first, he paid little attention to the occasional disappearance of a tool, but he started to believe the local rumors when four hammers disappeared in a single afternoon from within the locked house.

George Doesn't Rock

DeCapria was working late one night on the exterior of the Warren House. He had turned on a radio playing loud rock music inside the house to keep him company, but abruptly, the radio ceased playing. He thought something had happened to the broadcast, but the radio never came back on. He went inside and found the radio had been manually switched off. DeCapria switched the radio on again and returned to work. Minutes later, the radio was again turned off.

"It was George," he informed the *Atlanta Journal Constitution* in February 1985. "I thought, hey, if he doesn't like the music, I'll let it go."

Those who are familiar with the Warren House attribute these phenomena to George, a fourteen-year-old, one-armed Union soldier from Ohio who was never able to return home.

"I've heard him," stated DeCapria's co-worker Mike Childress. "There are weird noises you can't explain. It feels like someone is watching over your shoulder sometimes." The workers believe George eventually became accustomed to their presence.

On numerous occasions, the men heard footsteps on the staircase when they were the only living beings in the house. Those footfalls led to the third-story death room.

DeCapria and Childress carefully removed seven layers of wallpaper to reveal penciled names of soldiers who served in the Ohio Volunteer Militia and the date September 2, 1864, the day after the battle.

"We have heard stories about ghosts in the house," revealed American Home Health Care executive assistant Andrea Bruce when the office opened in 1986. As a result, they "had a medium come to the house." Bruce held a séance during which she learned of grand parties hosted in the house before the Civil War, including a great wedding in 1859. One of the frequently sighted ghosts is a woman clad in a beautiful wedding dress who appears at the top of the stairs. "We found it all hard to believe," Bruce said, but that was before she discovered George's hatred of modern music.

"When we put you on hold, the radio comes on," she revealed to an *Atlanta Journal Constitution* reporter. "Someone called and said, 'The radio is not working.'"

The radio, part of a clock mechanism, was kept behind a heavy filing cabinet that required two people to move.

"We looked and the radio had been turned off," Bruce said. "It's in my office and no one had been in there. We have no idea how that happened. We kidded that it was George. Apparently he doesn't like the kind of music we play."

"I love it," Bruce said of their spirit guest. "I think it's great. He's a nice ghost and he never bothers anybody."

Psst, Don't Tell the Patients, They'll Think We're Crazy

A decade passed as the Warren House became the Fairview Day Hospital, and the ghosts became even more active. Some of the sophisticated doctors refused to discuss the topic, but others accepted the ghosts as part of their workplace. The house is "visited by spirits" stated Sheila Bremer to the *Atlanta Journal Constitution* in October 1996.

"I think there are at least four ghosts here," the accountant continued, "and I've experienced two of them." One of her personal ghosts, an older woman who is scented rather than sighted, was thought to be a maid detected in a downstairs kitchen. Bremer was showing guests the house when she smelled a heavy lilac perfume that "seemed to follow me down the hall." However, staffers wisely kept the ghost stories to themselves. "It's not good to traumatize the patients," Bremer advised.

Two ghosts were Civil War soldiers. A fourteen-year-old girl spotted one, a "white shadowy figure" in nineteenth-century dress, Bremer said. "She said, 'Can't you see it? There's a man standing up there in the upstairs window.' I thought at the time it might be one of the doctors. But I went inside, and everybody had gone home. Nobody was there." Perhaps it was George.

A red-bearded, uniformed soldier has been observed sitting in an office upstairs, looking out the window at the nearby Confederate cemetery. Perhaps he is buried there or on the grounds. Several people have reported sighting a soldier holding a candle and peering out a window.

"Doctors amputated limbs of wounded soldiers and threw them out the window," Bremer said. "The story is there was a pile of arms and legs on the ground five or six feet deep." Limbs were amputated in the room that soldiers decorated with their names.

Not all the entities inhabiting the structure are benevolent. An angry ghost shoved one employee down a flight of stairs, but thankfully, a friendly ghost broke her fall at the bottom.

Some believed the stories, an employee said, but others "think you're crazy."

The building was purchased in 1992 by psychologist Jack Farrar and his lawyer wife, Laura, who planned their renovations.

"Last time there was a renovation here, the house's ghosts didn't like it one bit," Jack said. "The people working Home Health said their tools were hidden all over the house and that the radio station was changed from rock to country."

He had hopes for the new renovations, saying, "The ghosts shouldn't mess with us this time. All the changes we're making are good."

In 1994, Laura and a friend were downstairs when they heard footsteps on the stairs. They thought it was her husband, but he descended several minutes later and said he had been in a different part of the house. The three searched the structure but found no living beings.

"I will never spend a night in that house," she declared, even though she was not certain it was haunted.

"I've just been named the president of the Georgia Psychological society," Jack Farrar told Jeffery Scott, an *Atlanta Journal Constitution* reporter, on Halloween 1996. "I really don't want to talk about ghosts."

"Every time I pass the Warren House," said Mark Pollard, a Civil War reenactor, "it's like it's reaching out and telling me something new."

"If anything around here is going to be haunted," said Peter Bonner, a local tour guide, "it would be that house up on the hill."

The Atlanta Ghost Hunters spent three evenings in the Warren House. On October 22, 2006, hunters Cookie and Andy captured an appropriate EVP from the house, "I want peace and I want it now." That night, the team was distributed through the house "in silent mode." Andy and Cookie were alone in a second-floor room, whispering quietly when, "Suddenly, something 'swipes' across the empty space on the couch right next to Andy and an unknown item bounces across the floor several times. They have no idea what it was. That night's entire team scoured the floor looking for even the smallest item that could have made that noise…to no avail. We found nothing." The commotion occurred on the bare, wooden Civil War–era floor.

On the final night, October 26, 2006, Albert, Andy, Scott, Kevin and Willie were intently examining the ancient fireplace in the Signature Room when "the door to the room just closed. It had been in the same position opened entirely up the frame's wall the entire time…We tried to find its center of balance, and it was almost flush to the wall. There is simply no explanation." Investigation found its balance point to be at the wall—it could not have swung unaided.

At one point Andy "mentioned hearing a dragging sound, then the voice recorder suddenly stopped recording and started playing." Orbs were photographed at that time, including one that seemed on "an intelligent path of travel" and rendezvoused with a second orb.

The Atlanta Ghost Hunters returned on February 27, 2009, and recorded several EVPs: "Get out of here," "I won't let him," "I lost my finger," "hurts" and "go with us."

Across the highway from the Warren House is the Patrick Cleburne Confederate Cemetery, where casualties from the battle of Jonesboro are buried. It is also reputed to be haunted, with good orb photographs taken there. Jan Doolittle Page caught an orb in motion during daylight, several additional ones that night and, a week later, two more daylight anomalies. "These men will show for you day or night," she bragged of the Jonesboro dead.

On the anniversary of the Battle of Jonesboro, August 31 and September 1, residents hear drums and gunshots in the night and Confederate and Federal soldiers parade through certain houses, the Confederate Cemetery and the battlefield. Blood-spattered walls and mysterious bullet holes have appeared in homes.

The Carnes House (154 North McDonough Street, 1850s) was constructed by Stephen Carnes, who had a wagon and carriage shop behind the house, where he also constructed the gingerbread trim for his home. He built wooden coffins for the Confederate army and, reportedly, for the Union army after Sherman occupied Jonesboro, which kept his home safe from destruction. Following the war, the State of Georgia hired him to gather the Rebel dead from the Jonesboro battlefield and reinter them in the Confederate Cemetery. It is thought that he embalmed the dead in the only upstairs room.

The Carnes house is currently occupied by Bouvette Properties, a real estate firm. Ed Bouvette says that in 2001, a former employee was working in the house late one night, alone in the antebellum structure, when she

The Jonesboro Confederate Cemetery occupies part of the battlefield.

heard scratching, pounding and other sounds from the embalming room. Gathering her courage, the woman approached the long flight of stairs leading to the second floor. At the bottom of the steep stairs, the sounds intensified, and as she looked up the stairs, she clearly saw a man, dressed in a Confederate uniform, standing on the second floor gazing back at her. She was horrified as the figure motioned her to join him upstairs. The lady raced out and called the police, who of course found nothing. The current owners have named their friendly ghost Walter, believing he inhabits the upstairs, which they call "Walter's Room."

The Henry Ghost Hunters initially arrived on the night of October 28, 2006. Investigators Albert and Andy found the home normal until they carried audio and visual equipment to Walter's lair upstairs, where "we were stunned by a loud scratching in the walls," they wrote. "We were pretty frozen for a moment," then they set up their equipment. Following a brief calm, the scratching resumed and "then turned to banging in the walls. There were at times scratching in two sides of the room." The men felt "a serious energy in the air" that left both "very uncomfortable."

Three investigators—Andy, Claudia and Caroline—returned November 1, 2006, and decided to conduct an experiment. It has been theorized that carrying on a conversation in a foreign language provokes more EVPs, so they spoke German. The opposite effect resulted, as they wrote, "There was a totally different feeling the entire night. There wasn't the slightest creak in the home." Several orbs were photographed.

The Spooks of Stately Oaks

Stately Oaks, an 1839 plantation house and its original detached kitchen and other outbuildings, has been moved from its original four-hundred-acre site to the north of Jonesboro and restored. The structure, a landmark for Sherman's armies and thought to have been a field hospital during the fighting, and the surrounding fields, which were campgrounds during the fighting around Jonesboro, are open for tours.

Brenda Pillatzki, a docent at Stately Oaks, has never seen a ghost around the old house, but she has witnessed many doors opening and shutting themselves and has heard innumerable mysterious footsteps.

Ted Key, chairman of Historical Jonesboro, heard light footsteps on the wooden floors echoing in the house as he worked late and alone.

Two other volunteers also experienced the sounds of footfalls and the closing of doors while each was alone in the building. One night, Key locked the building and started for his car. Glancing back, he saw the shadow of a person standing at the front window. Fearing an intruder was in the house, Key enlisted the aid of volunteers holding a meeting in a small building behind Stately Oaks, and the men searched the historic mansion. They found it to be empty of the breathing.

Lovejoy

Just to the south of Jonesboro, at Lovejoy, where the Confederate army retreated after losing Atlanta, a ghost train is heard, perhaps the last to escape from the city, and spirit soldiers have been spotted in residences.

Douglas County

The Gray Ghost on Gray Road

Near Douglasville is Gray Road, a short lane named for a Civil War officer. His equestrian spirit has been encountered around an old barn in the woods, ordering trespassers to leave his property. They invariably obey.

And the Horse You Rode in On

Chester H. Heath spent his working years at Lockheed in Marietta. His passion was hunting treasure and Civil War artifacts. He was following (running) Indian trail signs in April 1971 when he took a Polaroid picture of a trail tree. It developed with "a white disc" in the center. His wife informed him that he had captured a spirit. After years of photographing such sites, he was suddenly able to record the images of long deceased Native Americans. In his book *Spirit Photographs at Treasure Sites*, Heath related the story of a Confederate soldier who lived in Douglas County and was visiting home on leave when Sherman advanced through the area in 1864. The officer captured five Federals as they rustled cattle and hanged them from a tree. When Union forces discovered the bodies, they pursued the Confederate and killed him with a shot to the head during a shootout at Pine Log Mountain.

When Heath accompanied a friend to search for a treasure in that area, "I told the owner of the land that I sure would like to get a picture of the Confederate officer in his uniform as he sat on the back of his horse," he wrote. Although the owner explained that the spirit was evil, Heath assured him that did not matter. "So I snapped the picture with a 35mm camera, and there appeared a black horse coming through the pines." The horse also appeared on a second photo.

ELSEWHERE IN METRO ATLANTA

Smiling for the Camera

In a metro Atlanta antique store that wishes to remain anonymous, a number of employees have sighted the image of a Confederate soldier. Ghost hunter GrayGhost learned that it has been seen by the light of day during business hours and after closing at midnight. He has investigated the property several times, concentrating on a spot where the apparition appears. On the night of October 7, 2004, about 11:00 p.m., he took "several photos of a partial torso and full body anomaly" in the haunted area. The figure, arms folded in front of his body, stares directly into the camera. As GrayGhost described it, "There is a very clear apparition of a man wearing a wide brim, flat top, slouch hat and a long frock coat." Several female spirits are also visible.

His Invisible Blue Friend

John Dantzler, whose father was the minister of a small church, lived in a town near Atlanta when he was four years old. He had gotten up one night to sleep with his parents when he saw a man walk through a closed window into his room. He remembered no fear and "just stood there, looking up at the man in my room."

"Go back to bed," the man instructed John, and he did. The ghost sat in a rocker and talked to the boy until he fell asleep. This apparition, which Dantzler called "my blue friend," appeared several times. He informed his mother, who was amused by the stories of his "invisible friend."

Some time later, John's mother was reading him a book about the Civil War. When he saw a photograph of a Confederate soldier, he said the blue man wore a uniform like that but obviously a Federal version. His mother "was amazed when I compared the uniform items in the picture with the items I remember the man wearing," adult John related.

Union Officer Still on Duty

A metropolitan Atlantan known as One2loveB4 entered his basement at 1:00 a.m. to find "a war officer dressed in blue staring at me." The contemporary man screamed and left quickly and has only returned in the company of his parents.

The number and variety of metropolitan Atlanta's Civil War ghosts are ever increasing.

PART III
CIVIL WAR REINCARNATION

A Latter-Day John B. Gordon

In May 1991, Jeffery Keene, a decorated fire fighter from Connecticut, and his wife were on vacation when they entered Sharpsburg, Maryland, to shop for antiques. Although Keene had no previous interest in the Civil War, he felt a need to visit the nearby Antietam battlefield. One of the most dramatic portions of the battlefield is the Sunken Road, where Keene listened to a taped narrative and walked along the lane. Suddenly, a "wave of grief, sadness and anger washed over me," Keene wrote later. He had difficulty breathing, and tears coursed down his face. After the experience passed, he was left exhausted, shaken and mystified. What had happened to him?

Keene and his wife visited a gift shop before leaving Sharpsburg. There, he purchased a magazine devoted to the battle, but he did not open it for over a year. When Keene finally started reading the magazine, he was struck by the physical resemblance between himself and a photograph of Confederate general John B. Gordon of Georgia. He was amazed to learn that Gordon had suffered multiple wounds in the Sunken Road and almost died.

Keene may be reaching here, but he counts September 9 as significant because that was the day Robert E. Lee issued the orders that culminated in the pivotal battle at Antietam. Keene's birthday is September 9, and fifteen years before his experience at Antietam, on September 9, 1977, he was rushed to the emergency room because of severe facial pain. Its cause was never determined, but one of Gordon's painful wounds at Antietam was to his face.

Keene also sees similarities with Gordon in their styles of writing, preferred mode of dress, general personality and scars that reflect the general's numerous battle wounds. He feels that Gordon's leadership style matches the way he directs firefighting crews. It is also suggested that groups of people can be reincarnated together in different lives, and there is a possibility that some of Gordon's soldiers may be Keene's firemen in this life.

John B. Gordon was the general who actually led the surrender of the Army of Northern Virginia at Appomattox. Keene was at a Civil War museum where artifacts from the surrender were displayed. Gazing at a print of the surrender, Keene knew the flag depicted was not the actual one used in the ceremony, but he spotted what he thought was the original flag in a display. Museum staff acknowledged Keene's insight—the actual flag was in a case, and the flag in the print was from a later era.

Keene's book on the topic, *Someone Else's Yesterday*, was published in 2003.

In My Lives

J. Marc Williams of Alaska recorded his past life experiences with the website Past Life Memory Bank. During past-life regression therapy administered by a hypnotist, Williams recalled growing up near Savannah in the 1840s. He enlisted in the Sixteenth Georgia Infantry and fought in Virginia with Stonewall Jackson in 1862's Valley Campaign and at Antietam, where he was wounded. He received a battlefield commission to the rank of captain and participated in the war's great eastern battles. At Cold Harbor, where U.S. Grant's Federals were slaughtered, Williams recalled "that the dead lay in heaps" before his position. He and a sergeant left the trenches to move the bodies so their men would have clear fields of fire. While reentering the works, "I was hit from the rear by three minie bullets," he remembered. "I saw them exit my chest in a bloody mess."

A woman who submitted her experiences to the same website recalled more and more pieces of her past life as she grew older. What she remembers today was life as a young woman on a Georgia plantation from just before the Civil War to the middle of the conflict. She had long black hair, pale skin, and an *S* name, perhaps Samantha, Sarah or Suzanne. According to her images, she was raised by loving slaves as a child and was not of interest to her family until she was older. She hated the way the slaves were treated and was horrified by the sight of her father viciously beating one.

S fell in love with an older, educated neighbor named Andrew who had a scheme to assist slaves in Mississippi. Andrew asked her to accompany him, but she could not.

After the war started, her family hosted several Confederates in their house. She liked one of them, and her father persuaded her to marry him. She and the soldier enjoyed one leave home before he was killed in combat. That loss drove *S* into "extreme despair."

CONCLUSION

Atlanta has long been called the Phoenix City, for it has truly risen from the ashes of the death and destruction of the Civil War. It has become a great American city and a leader of the southeast region in every aspect. Despite the changing nature of metropolitan Atlanta, its dramatic history has not been forgotten. Battlefields, sacred cemeteries and historic buildings remain as symbols of past valor and sacrifice. If anyone should dare forget, the sprints of the past will rise up as a reminder.

APPENDIX

Haunted Places Open to the Public

Kennesaw Mountain National Battlefield Park
900 Kennesaw Mountain Drive
Kennesaw, Georgia 30152
(770) 427-4686; fax (770) 528-8398
www.nps.gov/keno

Southern Museum
2829 Cherokee Street
Kennesaw, Georgia 30144
(770) 427-2117; fax (770) 421-8485
www.southernmuseum.org

Marietta Museum of History
1 Depot Street, Suite 200
Marietta, Georgia 30060
(770)-794-5710; fax (770) 794-5733
http://www.mariettahistory.org
info@mariettahistory.org

The Public House (formerly J. Christopher's Restaurant)
605 Atlanta Street
Roswell, Georgia 30075
(770) 640-5548

Historic Oakland Foundation
248 Oakland Avenue Southeast
Atlanta, Georgia 30312
Cemetery: (404) 658-6019; Foundation: (404) 688-2107
www.oaklandcemetery.com

Warren House
102 West Mimosa Drive
Jonesboro, Georgia 30236
Private

Stately Oaks Plantation
100 Carriage Lane
P.O. Box 922
Jonesboro, Georgia 30237
(770) 473-0197
http://www.historicaljonesboro.org

The Village Inn
992 Ridge Avenue
Stone Mountain, Georgia 30083
Private

Ghost Tours

Ghost tours have been a popular form of historical entertainment for many years, and they often incorporate paranormal tales relating to the Civil War. Roswell has an established tour, and other cities occasionally sponsor them. Ghost tour operators, like ghost hunting organizations, rise and fall frequently, so check to see what is currently available in your area of interest, particularly around Halloween.

BIBLIOGRAPHY

BOOKS

Alan, Ian. *Georgia Ghosts: They Are Among Us*. Los Angeles, CA: Sweetwater Press, 2005.

Asfar, Dan, and Edrick That. *Ghost Stories of the Civil War*. Alberta, Canada: Ghost House Books, 2003.

Avena, Dianna. *Roswell: History, Haunts, and Legends*. Charleston, SC: The History Press, Haunted America, 2007.

Barber, Christian A. *Spirits of Georgia's Southern Crescent*. Atglen, PA: Schiffer, 2008.

Belanger, Jeff. *Ghosts of War: Restless Spirits of Soldiers, Spies, and Saboteurs*. Franklin Lakes, NJ: New Page Books, 2006.

Bender, William N. *Haunted Atlanta and Beyond*. Toccoa, GA: Currahee Books, 2008.

Brown, Alan. *Ghost Hunters of the South*. Jackson: University Press of Mississippi, 2006.

———. *Haunted Georgia: Ghosts and Strange Phenomena of the Peach State*. Mechanicsburg, PA: Stackpole Books, 2008.

———. *Stories from the Haunted South*. Jackson: University Press of Mississippi, 2004.

Christian, Reese. *Ghosts of Atlanta: Phantoms of the Phoenix City*. Charleston, SC: The History Press, Haunted America, 2008.

Coleman, Christopher, K. *Ghosts and Haunts of the Civil War*. Nashville, TN: Rutledge Hill Press, 1999.

———. *Strange Tales of the Dark and Bloody Ground*. Nashville, TN: Rutledge Hill Press, 1998.

Duffey, Barbara. *Angels and Apparitions: True Ghost Stories from the South*. Eatonton, GA: Elysian Publishing Company, 1996.

———. *Banshees, Bugles and Belles: True Georgia Ghost Stories*. Berryville, VA: Rockbridge Publishing Company, 1999.

———. *Miracles from Heaven*. Eatonton, GA: Elysian Publishing Company, 1998.

Guide to Haunted Places of the Civil War. Columbus, OH: *Blue & Gray Magazine*, 1996.

Heath, Chester H. *Spirit Photographs at Treasure Sites*. New York: Vantage Press, 1976.

Keene, Jeffrey J. *Someone Else's Yesterday*. Nevada City, CA: Blue Dolphin Publishing, Inc., 2003.

Key, William. *The Battle of Atlanta*. Atlanta, GA: Peachtree Publishers, Inc, 1981.

Kotarski, Georgiana C. *Ghosts of the Southern Tennessee Valley*. Winston-Salem, NC: John F. Blair Publishers, 2006.

Miles, Jim. *Civil War Sites in Georgia*. Nashville, TN: Rutledge Hill Press, 1996.

———. *Fields of Glory*. Nashville, TN: Cumberland House, 2002.

Morrison, Nannette. *Echoes of Valor*. Charlottesville, VA: Morrison, 1994.

Norman, Michael, and Beth Scott. *Haunted America*. New York: Tor, 1994.

Roberts, Nancy. *Georgia Ghosts*. Winston-Salem, NC: John F. Blair Publishers, 1997.

Sallee, Scott E., ed. "Camp Talk." *Blue & Gray*, October 2000.

Sanders, Michael. *Strange Tales of the Civil War*. Shippensburg, PA: Burd Street Press, 2001.

Spaeth, Frank, ed. *Phantom Army of the Civil War*. Secaucus, NJ: Castle Books, 1997.

Taylor, Troy. *Spirits of the Civil War*. Alton, IL: Whitechapel Productions Press, 1999.

Toney, B. Keith. *Battlefield Ghosts*. Berryville, VA: Rockbridge Publishing, 1997.

Turnage, Sheila. *Haunted Inns of the Southeast*. Winston-Salem, NC: John F. Blair Publishers, 2001.

Underwood, Corinna. *Haunted History: Atlanta and North Georgia*. Atglen, PA: Schiffer Publishing, 2008.

Visions of Ghost Armies, Real-Life Encounters with War-Torn Spirits, from the Files of FATE *Magazine*. New York: Barnes & Noble, 2003.

Walls, Kathleen. *Georgia's Ghostly Getaways*. Global Authors Publications, 2003.

Wangler, Chris. *Ghost Stories of Georgia, True Tales of Ghostly Hauntings*. Auburn, WA: Long Pine Publishing International, 2006.

Winer, Richard, and Nancy Osborn Ishmael. *Haunted Houses*. New York: Bantam, 1979.

———. *More Haunted Houses*. New York: Bantam, 1983.

VIDEO

The Unexplained. "Civil War Ghosts." A&E Television Network, 1999.

About the Author

Jim Miles is author of seven books of the Civil War Explorer Series (*Fields of Glory*, *To the Sea*, *Piercing the Heartland*, *Paths to Victory*, *A River Unvexed*, *Forged in Fire* and *The Storm Tide*), *Civil War Sites in Georgia* and two books titled *Weird Georgia*. The History Book Club has featured five of his books, and he has been historical adviser to two History Channel documentaries. He has a bachelor's degree in history and a master's of education degree from Georgia Southwestern State University in Americus. He taught high school American history for thirty-one years. Over a span of forty years, Jim has logged tens of thousands of miles exploring every nook and cranny in Georgia and Civil War sites throughout the country. He lives in Warner Robins, Georgia, with his wife, Earline.

ENJOY A SNEAK PEEK FROM JIM MILES'S

CIVIL WAR GHOSTS OF CENTRAL GEORGIA AND SAVANNAH

Fighting Ghosts

Savannah was vulnerable to approach from the Atlantic Ocean via a number of waterways. One of the most important was the Ogeechee River, a valuable shelter for blockade runners. To protect this route, the river was obstructed by Fort McAllister, a nine-gun earthen fort designed and constructed by Captain John McCready. Major John B. Gallie commanded the garrison of two hundred when the Union navy decided to destroy the position. On January 27, 1863, the ironclad monitor *Montauk*, accompanied by several wooden ships, steamed upriver and unleashed a five-hour bombardment. Despite the damage caused by sixty-one fifteen-inch, 450-pound explosive shells, the fort survived. At night, the garrison swarmed over the dirt and sand walls, easily repairing gaping holes.

The *Montauk* returned on February 1 and took position less than one thousand yards away. Throughout the bombardment Major Gallie ventured from one gun position to another, encouraging his gunners during the frightening attack. He chose as his personal position an eight-inch Columbiad because it was closest to the attackers. It and a thirty-two-pounder rifled cannon were the only pieces that could reach the *Montauk*, and in turn, the monitor concentrated its fire on those guns. A shell fragment wounded Gallie in the head, but he refused to go to the safety of a bombproof. The earthworks protecting his weapon were chewed to pieces, but the piece continued to fire, even when a Union

Confederate major Gallie was killed at his post during a Union bombardment of Fort McAllister. His headless apparition has been seen here.

fifteen-inch shell decapitated the major. Again Fort McAllister survived, and that night, the men repaired the massive destruction to the fort.

One month later, March 3, 1863, the Union navy returned, determined to subdue the stubborn Confederate fortification. Three ironclads came this time—*Passaic*, *Nahant* and *Patapsco*—accompanied by three mortar schooners and two wooden gunboats. The attack lasted seven hours, but McAllister suffered only one casualty: Tom Cat, the garrison's black cat mascot, killed while racing across the parapets. The animal, deeply mourned by the garrison, was mentioned in the official report of the battle. He was buried within the fort and is today commemorated by a historical marker.

The lack of results forced the Union navy to abandon its plan for reducing Fort McAllister. Nearly two years passed before William T. Sherman reached Savannah with his sixty-thousand-man army. He surrounded the city but needed to eliminate Fort McAllister to allow resupply and support by naval ships waiting offshore. On December 13, 1864, Sherman sent four thousand infantrymen against the fort's two hundred defenders. The Union advance was magnificent in the face of the opposing artillery, but the defenders covered themselves with glory. They fought furiously until Union forces smothered the fort and every Confederate was individually subdued. Sherman, observing nearby, called it "the handsomest thing I have seen in the war." Many Confederate and Union soldiers died in the brief battle.

Roger Durham, former director of Fort McAllister, never saw a ghost, but confided, "There are stories." When Henry Ford purchased a nearby plantation and had the fortification reconstructed during the 1930s, he asked workers to sleep on the grounds at night to prevent vandalism and theft of historic artifacts.

"Well, they never did spend a full night here!" Durham told Margaret DeBolt, author of *Savannah Spectres and Other Strange Tales*. "Sometime during the first night they were gone, and after that they were out of here every day at sundown. There were stories that they had heard strange sounds and so forth." He added, "Let's just say that it gets very dark and very quiet out there on the earthworks at night."

One February in the 1960s, park employees were working in the fort, cutting grass and doing general upkeep, when they noticed an abrupt,

In December 1864, thousands of Union troops overwhelmed Fort McAllister, but some of its faithful defenders, and the garrison cat, remain in spirit.

eerie silence accompanied by a sudden chilling sensation. Looking toward the remounted eight-inch Columbiad at Major Gallie's position, they spotted a headless man hovering above the earthworks. The apparition was clad in a blue militia uniform marked on the sleeves with officer's braid. After facing (figuratively, of course) the river for several minutes, it disappeared. The incident occurred at the same time on the anniversary of the day that Gallie died.

In *Ghost Stories of Georgia*, Chris Wangler tells of a North Carolina man who visited Fort McAllister in 2002. Hearing shouting, he thought a child was being disciplined but then realized that what he heard was a male voice shouting instructions to an artillery crew, culminating in the command, "Fire!" As he approached the Columbiad, he saw a hazy image of a man wearing an officer's uniform crouched at the artillery piece. As he walked forward, the apparition disappeared. Enquiring at the museum, the witness was told the story of Major Gallie.

A man with the Internet name Georgia Rebel snapped a number of photos around Fort McAllister, hoping something strange would register. His most unusual picture was taken inside the restored bombproof, where at one point, his camera malfunctioned. In the hospital portion of the facility, a ghostly figure is framed between two timbers. A careful examination shows what looks like the face, shoulders, trunk and legs of a man with a cartridge box at his waist.